Michele Evans'
SENSATIONAL SALADS

Michele Evans'
SENSATIONAL SALADS

Main Course Salads for Every Season

NAL BOOKS

NEW AMERICAN LIBRARY

A DIVISION OF PENGUIN BOOKS USA INC., NEW YORK
PUBLISHED IN CANADA BY
PENGUIN BOOKS CANADA LIMITED, MARKHAM, ONTARIO

NAL BOOKS TRADEMARK REG. U.S. PAT. OFF. AND FOREIGN COUNTRIES
REGISTERED TRADEMARK—MARCA REGISTRADA
HECHO EN KINGSPORT, TN

SIGNET, SIGNET CLASSIC, MENTOR, ONYX, PLUME,
MERIDIAN and NAL BOOKS are published *in the United States* by
New American Library, a division of Penguin Books USA Inc., 1633 Broadway,
New York, New York 10019, *in Canada* by Penguin Books Canada Limited,
2801 John Street, Markham, Ontario L3R 1B4

LIBRARY OF CONGRESS CATALOGING-IN-PUBLICATION DATA
Evans, Michele.
[Sensational salads]
Michele Evans' sensational salads.
p.   cm.
Includes index.
ISBN 0-453-00658-2
1. Salads.   2. Entrées (cookery)   3. Cookery (Salad dressing)
I. Title.   II.Title: Sensational salads.
TX740.E83   1989
641.8'3—dc19   88-35959
                                                                CIP

First Printing, May, 1989
1 2 3 4 5 6 7 8 9
PRINTED IN THE UNITED STATES OF AMERICA

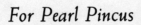

For Pearl Pincus

CONTENTS

INTRODUCTION

Main course salads represent an important culinary and cultural change in the way America eats. Today's main course salads have become distinct dining pleasures that play a major role in our meals at home and in restaurants everywhere. They have gained new attention and increased popularity as they have become more innovative and sophisticated dishes.

Much of today's salad renaissance stems from a renewed interest in regional American cooking—Californian, Southern, and Cajun—as well as a continuing openness to international influences such as Chinese, Mexican, Italian, French, Japanese, East Indian, Mediterranean, and Caribbean. Cooking techniques and harmonious food combinations have been borrowed from all these cuisines and successfully adapted to salad-making. Special food products from these regions have become readily available in local food markets, as has an increasing abundance of first-rate ingredients throughout the year, especially the vegetables, herbs, and fruits that figure prominently in salads.

Equally important, a new generation of skilled and demanding cooks and consumers insist on excellence and creativity in all their food. These high standards are supported by the growing national interest in fitness, diet, and nutrition, which has positioned salads high on everyone's list of *the right foods*. Today's nutritional buzz word is *light*, and salads have become synonymous with lightness at the table. Not all salads are low in calories, depending on the quantities of oils, mayonnaise, cheese, nuts, beans, and other high-fat ingredients used, but some of that caloric consumption is offset by the fact that smaller quantities of these ingredients are used in salads than would find their way into traditional heavier dishes. Regardless of the calorie count, almost any salad is more healthful than a high-fat content meat dish that has been sautéed or fried, other fried foods, or recipes rich in butter and cream sauces.

Most important of all, perhaps, is that well-balanced and thoughtfully prepared salads taste great and are tremendously satisfying. Salads are usually uncomplicated and simple to make. Many salads actually improve in flavor when prepared in advance, and since time is so crucial in today's busy schedules and lives, this is a valuable asset in meal-planning.

Main course salads are also universally appealing because of their enormous variety and scope. Salads are no longer simply greens mixed with a few other ingredients and a dressing; the possibilities for salad invention are limitless.

Virtually any food, whether as a chief ingredient or a subtle component, can be a candidate for a main course salad, from vegetables, fruits, pastas, potatoes, rices, grains, nuts, seafood, meat and poultry, beans and other legumes, and eggs and cheeses to fresh herbs and spices. Today's wide selection of vinegars and oils for complementing dressings and sauces extends the possibilities even further.

Salad bars have become part of the salad transformation. The original salad bar offered tomato wedges, sliced cucumbers, green pepper, celery and carrot sticks, crumbled bacon, and radishes accompanied by a large bowl of iceberg and romaine lettuce pieces and served with the three basic dressings: French, Italian, and blue cheese. Now salad bars display a dazzling array of choices, from alfalfa sprouts, sugar snap peas, artichoke hearts, yellow pear-shaped tomatoes, tiny young zucchini, other "new" or "baby" vegetables, jalapeño peppers, arugula, endive, oakleaf lettuce, or mache to a variety of prepared seafoods and meats.

Catering and carry-out food establishments are in the forefront in developing wonderful salads. Plain tunafish salad has been elevated by the addition of curry powder, currants, apples, pineapple, fresh grated orange rind, and mint. Oriental sesame oil, fried shallot slivers, and julienne strips of snow pea pods bring a new dimension to chicken salad, and new versions of pasta salads are constantly appearing, including every conceivable food from sun-dried tomatoes, braised cabbage and crumbled sweet sausage, tahini paste and peanut butter to caviar.

Salads today can be mixed, composed, or what I call "free form." Their composition is based on a delicate and harmonious balance of flavor, texture, color, and design. The new main course salad might focus on delicate mixed greens enhanced with slices of warm duck breast and sauerkraut with a raspberry vinaigrette and crisp skin cracklings, or circles of sliced scallops and grapefruit sections with a hazelnut dressing, garnished with slivered endive leaves. Both are recipes you will find in this book.

Yesterday's traditional salads can still be appreciated, but our more sophisticated palates demand a refinement and elevation. For example, a Chef Salad today can be made more enticing by replacing the strips of turkey breast and Swiss cheese with slices of beef tenderloin and Brie, and the Thousand Island dressing with a creamy Gorgonzola or Roquefort dressing.

Moreover, yesterday's premise that salads were limited to the warm weather months no longer applies. Salads are now a celebration of all seasons, limited only by the availability of fresh seasonal ingredients. Summer salads can be lighter than ever, and cooler-weather salads can be hearty without actually being heavy. Similarly, salad dressings and sauces can vary with the season. And both salads and salad dressings today can be served warm or hot.

There are many meal-in-one salads in this collection, like Paella Salad, Tabouli with Minced Lamb, and Gruyère, Celery, and Smoked Chicken Salad, but any meal must balance out, whether it features as its main course a salad or any traditional entrée. For a meal featuring a main course salad, a full menu is easily created by adding side dishes which can range from soup, edible garnishes, and vegetables, to canapés or finger sandwiches or selections from the enormous variety of breads available today, followed by dessert, if desired. Menu suggestions are given with many of the recipes in the book.

Some favorite salads that aren't substantial enough to qualify as a main course salad can be elevated to that status by the careful selection and addition of a complementing food—for example, a piquant Caesar Salad can be expanded into a main course salad by adding shrimp for flavor and protein. (Conversely, of course, any main course salad can become a first course, which will double the number of servings it yields.)

For the growing numbers of vegetarians, main course salads offer the possibility for extraordinary variety in meal-planning. There are many strictly vegetarian recipes among the recipes here, but vegetarians can also successfully eliminate meat, seafood, or dairy products and substitute tofu, beans, grains, or nuts, or any interesting combination to replace the protein.

Main course salads are also sensational for entertaining since they can be both easily made and versatile. Hosts and hostesses can offer guests an excellent choice of one or more interesting salads for a sit-down dinner, a buffet, a potluck dinner, a salad bar, or a picnic. In fact, entertaining with main course salads provides such a wide scope for creativity that I discuss it separately in the section that follows and give some sample menus at the end of the book.

As I see it, there are four basic requirements for successful salad-making: the use of the highest quality and freshest possible ingredients available, carefully prepared; a balanced complementing combination of textures, flavors, and colors; dressings and sauces with character and balance; and an attractive presentation.

Complementing combinations of textures, flavors, and colors, dressings, presentation and garnishes, and suggestions for accompanying dishes are addressed in the section on entertaining that follows.

Creative salads have never been more in fashion, and have never been more delicious. I predict that main course salads will continue to grow in popularity and stature, as a sensible and convenient style of cooking and eating. Rather than a trend, salads have evolved into the classic food of the moment and of the future.

Entertaining with Main Course Salads

Entertaining with main course salads is one of the most creative, satisfying, and easiest forms of entertaining, whether it's for two other couples or a dozen guests. The spectrum of salads that you can choose from is enormous. Both the salads and the particular style of dining that you select will depend on several factors: the season, the available ingredients, where and how you will dine, the number of guests, and the specific event. A variety of dining styles ranging from a summer picnic at the shore for six and a pasta salad tasting party for eight, to a New Year's Eve salad buffet for twelve and a box lunch in the park for four are illustrated in the Seasonal Menus at the end of the book. These menus are examples that are meant to spark your imagination and ignite your creative instincts so that you can develop your own salad menus for all types of occasions.

Simplicity is the best guideline to follow when entertaining, be it an elegant sit-down dinner or an outdoor barbecue. Nothing needs to be elaborate, exotic, or for that matter, excessively expensive. Organization and a well-planned and executed menu are the most important elements of entertaining.

A salad buffet is a delightful way to entertain. To organize a salad buffet for twelve, you might select three main course salads, making sure to balance the ingredients in the dishes by serving one meat or seafood salad, a complementing pasta, grain, rice, or potato salad, and a vegetable salad or salad based on greens. Consider the ingredients in all of the salads so that there is variety, and no duplication of foods. For example, all the salads shouldn't contain cheese, garlic, and parsley. However, if a food is cooked in one dish and served raw in another, then it's all right to use both, as the textures and flavors will differ. Cooking methods of individual dishes ought to differ when possible, too, for optimum taste pleasure.

The textures of the ingredients, the dressings, the size and cut or shapes of the foods, and the colors should also vary. For instance, all three salads should not have the same kind of dressings, or all have crunchy textures, or all be cut in the same shape (e.g., cubed), or all be the same color. A successful combination could be a shrimp salad with sun-dried tomatoes and basil in a creamy mayonnaise dressing, a firm sliced potato salad with a mustard vinaigrette, and an Oriental mixed vegetable salad of whole snow pea pods, sliced water chestnuts, julienne strips of carrots and zucchini, rings of red onion, and small whole mushrooms in a sesame oil and lemon dressing.

A friend of mine who entertains frequently always serves salad buffets for eight or more from her kitchen counter with two main course salads—a meat or seafood salad and a pasta, rice, or grain salad with green vegetables and herbs—and a contrasting vegetable on the side, which could be roasted yellow and red bell peppers sprinkled with vinegar, olive oil, and pepper, or any seasonal vegetable like corn on the cob with chili or cilantro butter, or baked acorn squash drizzled with a little honey. A basket of interesting bread is always part of her meal, too. It can be anything from French baguettes, whole wheat Italian or black bread, sesame breadsticks, sliced brioche, Armenian cracker bread, pita bread toasted with butter and herbs, or corn sticks.

Because the accompaniments to any meal are such a vital part of its success, I have included several recipes for some unusual additions: Parmesan Crostini, Johnnycakes,

Cheese and Green Chili Quesadillas, French Walnut Bread, Puff Pastry Crackers, and Fried Flour Tortilla Wedges, to name a few. Any of these and many others are an added highlight to a menu and make it more memorable.

At times main course salads will require a side dish beyond bread, rolls, or crackers in order to balance a menu, like my friend's contrasting vegetable. A classic chicken salad with green peas that is served with French bread and butter will be a fine light lunch, but for a more substantial dinner, the menu might begin with cream of corn soup. Since there are green peas in the salad, the accompanying vegetable served shouldn't be a green one. Fresh cooked carrots could accompany the main course salad or quickly sautéed cherry tomatoes. Or the accompanying dish could be a small serving of pasta such as orzo (rice-shaped pasta) with diced tomatoes in a pesto sauce.

For another kind of buffet for a salad lunch or dinner create your own special salad bar. For twelve guests, use three over-sized platters for the featured ingredients. One platter is for various greens: arugula, endive, young spinach leaves, shredded radicchio, romaine, chicory, and watercress arranged in rows or tossed together.

The second platter contains an assortment of fresh-cut vegetables, both raw and cooked: cooked chilled sliced new potatoes, asparagus lengths, whole string beans, cubed or sliced beets, baby artichoke hearts, shredded raw carrots, fennel or celery sliced on the diagonal, peeled and seeded cucumber slices, red radish halves, yellow and red cherry tomatoes, raw red pepper strips, and avocado cubes. Choose seasonal foods that will make appealing combinations.

The third platter is for meat and/or seafood: strips of rare fillet of beef, cold roasted chicken pieces or smoked turkey breast, lump crabmeat, shrimp, and mussels, or perhaps canned white-meat tunafish.

These three platters are placed on the buffet table followed by a selection of individual bowls filled with chopped hard-boiled eggs, small fried croutons, cubed feta cheese, fresh grated Parmesan cheese, cooked black beans, chopped walnuts, olives, cornichons, capers, anchovies, and such chopped fresh herbs as basil, dill, and tarragon.

Next comes the dressing. Only two dressings are really required, but they should be contrasting types—one oil-and-vinegar-based and one mayonnaise-based—for example, an excellent sharp vinaigrette and a creamy horseradish. Include lemon and lime wedges for those who are dieting, and cruets of virgin olive oil and red wine vinegar. And don't forget the peppermill.

Any of the interesting breads mentioned above, or biscuits and sweet butter, go well with the meal. When the main course salads are served cold or at room temperature, it is a nice touch to serve the accompanying rolls, biscuits, or bread hot or warm.

All of these foods described above needn't be included in the salad bar; an interesting assortment of top quality foods is all that's really required.

Dressings

Since it is the dressing that can make the salad, it will always need careful attention to achieve proper balance and character. We are fortunate today to be able to find so many different kinds of oils: fragrant olive, hazelnut, walnut, almond, avocado, and Oriental sesame, to name only a few. A high quality oil combined with a complementing vinegar, like balsamic or a choice of one of the many excellent fruit, herb, or wine vinegars, can produce the finest dressing imaginable.

Many other tasty ingredients can be incorporated into salad dressings effectively. Consideration should be given to mustards, shallots, garlic, Worcestershire sauce, lemon, lime, or grapefruit juices, cream, egg yolks, fresh herbs and spices, horseradish, anchovies, and even a dash of vanilla or almond essence or a liqueur or brandy.

There is no strict formula for making a fine vinaigrette or salad dressing because the strengths of the vinegars and pungency of the oils vary so much not only from company to company but from country to country in which they are manufactured. Tasting is the key to successful salad dressing, and to finding the products that best suit you.

It is generally agreed that a good dressing is one part vinegar to three parts oil. It has been my experience, however, that it is more like one part vinegar to two or two and a half parts oil if you like piquant dressings, as I do. Many French and Italian chefs use only a few tablespoons of oil to almost equal parts of mild vinegars, such as white wine, champagne, or lemon; stronger vinegars like balsamic and sherry wine will need more oil for a good balance.

Spices and almost any herb and a little lemon or lime juice added to mayonnaise result in a fabulous dressing. Mayonnaise-based dressings can be made with a good-quality commercial mayonnaise or with homemade. A classic homemade mayonnaise recipe is given on page 128. Mayonnaise-based dressings can be enlivened with basil and garlic, pureed tomatoes and ground saffron, or minced roasted red peppers and toasted sesame seeds. Also consider including minced chives, red onion, or Georgia's sweet Vidalia onion.

A variety of dressings appear throughout the recipes in the book, and a list can be found in the index. As you become more proficient at making delicious dressings, you can improvise and create your own.

Herbs

Fresh herbs are always preferable in salad-making for the subtle, more genuine flavor that they impart (fresh herbs should always be freshly chopped). However, since fresh seasonal herbs aren't always available, dried herbs are a satisfactory substitute. Because dried herbs have a more intense flavor, the rule of thumb for replacement is 1 teaspoon of dried herbs for 1 tablespoon of fresh. If the jarred dried herbs that you have are over two months old, they may have lost some of their strength, and a little more might be required. Taste and decide.

Presentation

Presentation is an important aspect of entertaining, and where salads are concerned, there is great latitude. Particular salads will often dictate how they will be served or arranged, so it is often the garnishes that will accent individual salads.

I have always preferred edible garnishes, such as fluted tomatoes or lemons, sliced oranges, bouquets of fresh herbs, or the simplicity of fresh greens. An occasional flower as a garnish is fine, but I recently attended a function where I was served a magnificent fruit and chicken salad presented on a platter adorned with gardenia blossoms. The sweet strong fragrance of the flowers was so potent that it overpowered the flavor of the food. I believe that food should look like food, not a floral arrangement, and should not be so artistically arranged that one feels uncomfortable scooping up a serving.

In serving food, use a variety of shapes and sizes of bowls and platters. They all shouldn't be round, but a combination of shapes: oval, rectangular, round, scalloped, etc. Use contrasting materials, too: wood, ceramic, glass, porcelain, or silver.

Never before has *how* a salad looked been more important. Consider the elements already discussed. Attractively presented food begins to satisfy the audience even before they taste it. The "look" of a salad represents the quality of the ingredients and the care taken in preparation of the dish. Arranging the salad as a finished dish is just as enjoyable and satisfying to the cook as it is to the audience, a factor which I feel is of considerable importance.

When we entertain, we want our guests to feel at ease and be tempted by inviting food. Beautifully presented main course salads allow the cook the option of advance preparation so that he or she can tend to guests, serve a marvelous meal, and enjoy the dinner as well.

Creating Your Own Salads

It shouldn't be forgotten that entertaining also includes the everyday meals for ourselves and our families. To make the daily duty more exciting, use this time to build up your own skills, and use your imagination. This is how I approach recipe development, which is for me unending, and it is often one of the most relaxing and enjoyable parts of my day. I examine a food that I want to use as a main salad ingredient—shrimp, for example. I decide to begin with a basic dressing of mayonnaise, lemon juice, chopped tarragon, and freshly grated pepper. It's simple, lovely, and it works. Because shrimp is costly, in the next recipe I test I'll cut the quantity of shrimp in half and balance out the dish with pasta, enhanced with fennel or celery and roasted red peppers, with a red wine vinegar and

olive oil dressing, seasoned with salt and pepper. If this proves too bland, I'll introduce bolder ingredients: minced anchovies, shredded arugula, minced garlic, and cocktail onions. (Now I realize that I've overdone it—no cocktail onions.)

To develop your own recipes, try variations on favorite recipes and classic dishes or adaptations of appealing ideas. A dish sampled in a restaurant or even foods grouped together in the market can be inspiration for recipes. For example, savoring a tostado in a Mexican restaurant, you might be struck with a concept of filling crusty tortilla shells with an unlikely seafood salad with rice instead of the usual beans, lettuce, cheese, scallions, and spiced ground meat. Recipe ideas come from everywhere if you are open to them and are on the lookout.

I find many new recipe ideas on trips. For me, one of the great joys of traveling is returning home and re-creating some of the exceptional dishes I sampled or trying out new ideas.

Welcome inspiration for salads often comes from leftovers. Using up leftovers is a great challenge for home cooks. Raw cauliflower is a great salad ingredient—mixed with cooked chicken, pork, beef, turkey, lamb, or seafood and a Roquefort dressing, you can't go wrong. If you have leftover black olives, or raisins, a few of either or both tossed into a salad could make a superb addition. As it happens, either the olives or raisins added to the cauliflower salad above works very well. Never add too much of a single ingredient or too many different ingredients, however, remembering that a salad must balance.

Your own and your family's tastes and food preferences will figure strongly in developing your own recipes. Favorite foods can be substituted in comparable quantities in many salad recipes, eliminating ingredients that you dislike, that are unavailable, or that you try to avoid for dietary reasons.

Cost and convenience realistically enter the picture when entertaining guests or feeding your own family. If, for example, you are partial to a certain veal recipe but aren't content with the cost of the main ingredient or don't want to make a trip to the market, by all means use cooked pork or roast chicken instead. A lobster salad with celery and a tartar sauce dressing is excellent prepared with shrimp or chicken instead of the lobster.

By applying your own inventive imagination to the recipes in this book you can more than triple the number of salads it contains.

BEAN, LENTIL, AND GRAIN SALADS

The first time that I sampled Tuscany's succulent white bean and tuna salad in Florence, the initial bite came as an exciting awakening. I hadn't expected it to be so rich, wonderfully aromatic, and substantial, or so addicting. Although the bean salad was part of an antipasto buffet of two dozen or so other offerings, served from a rolling cart at tableside, I found myself concentrating on it alone. I asked for a second helping and the waiter proceeded to spoon a generous portion of the pungent mixture over half of my dinner plate, adding a drizzle of dark green extra-virgin olive oil over the salad, and passing me the peppermill. I ate every morsel contentedly. That moment was the beginning of my love for robust, fragrant bean salads, an appreciation that soon included lentil and grain salads too.

Fresh beans or cooked dried beans are always preferable in a salad, though good-quality canned beans—drained and rinsed—will do if time or availability is a consideration. Even a humble three-bean salad can become quite special if fresh-cooked beans are used in interesting combinations, such as black, navy, and pinto beans. The addition of other ingredients like cooked chicken, scallions, whole corn kernels, and diced red pepper lends texture and complementary flavors. A thick emulsified dressing, composed of top-quality vinegar, olive oil, mustard, and chopped fresh herbs will give the necessary zest.

For a hearty cold-weather meal, try a moist, warm lentil salad with a vinaigrette dressing: top with sautéed sliced mushrooms and serve with warm biscuits. Chilled, this same salad, garnished with deviled egg salad and served with crusty French bread, makes a great warm weather entrée.

For main course salads with an interesting mix, look, and flavor, lentils can be combined with grains, such as wheat berries or couscous, or with rice.

Grains produce lovely, hearty, slightly nutty-tasting salads on their own as well. One that has recently come on the market in the United States is quinoa, a delicate, subtly flavored Peruvian grain which makes especially inviting, light, and attractive salads.

Bean, lentil, and grain main course salads are economical, nutritious, substantial, and delectable. They offer salad lovers unusual options, and are a vegetarian's delight.

ECIPES

Cannellini and Tuna Salad with Smoked Mozzarella

Mexican Bean Salad with Green Chili Dressing
and Pan Corn Bread

Black Bean and Crunchy Vegetable Salad

Marinated Bean Salad in Roast Beef Packages

Minestrone Salad with Tomato Vinaigrette

Molded Curried Couscous and Shrimp Salad

Lentil and Vegetable Salad with Spedini

Tabouli with Minced Lamb

Quinoa and Sesame Shrimp Salad

Wheat Berry Mediterranean Salad

Cannellini and Tuna Salad with Smoked Mozzarella

The basic recipe for classic white bean and tuna salad is superb and quite well known. Here is a slightly different herbed version, which introduces the new flavors of smoked mozzarella, yellow peppers, and black olives to an old favorite. Serve with crusty Italian bread and sweet butter.

2 cups dried cannellini beans, soaked in cool
   water overnight, drained, and rinsed
1 large yellow onion, quartered
1 teaspoon minced garlic
½ teaspoon dried sage
½ teaspoon dried thyme
6 sprigs parsley
1 bay leaf
1 tablespoon salt
3 tablespoons freshly squeezed lemon juice
6 tablespoons white wine vinegar
¾ cup virgin olive oil
Salt and freshly ground pepper to taste
2 6½-ounce cans solid white-meat tuna,
   drained and flaked
½ cup black olive slivers
2 stalks celery, thinly sliced
½ cup diced cored and seeded yellow bell
   pepper
½ cup diced red onion
2 tablespoons chopped fresh basil
3 tablespoons chopped fresh parsley (reserve
   1 tablespoon for garnish)
8 ounces smoked mozzarella (unsmoked
   mozzarella can be used)
18 cherry tomatoes, cut in half

Put the beans in a heavy 4- to 5-quart pot and cover them with 1½ inches of water. Add the onion, garlic, sage, thyme, parsley sprigs, bay leaf, and salt. Bring the water to a boil; immediately reduce the heat and simmer, stirring often, for about 2 hours, or until the beans are tender.

Drain the beans and discard the onion pieces, bay leaf, and parsley sprigs.

Transfer the beans to a large bowl. Combine the lemon juice, vinegar, and oil, and pour over the beans. Season well with salt and pepper and gently toss.

Add all the remaining ingredients, except for the reserved parsley and the mozzarella and cherry tomatoes, and combine gently.

Cool the salad for 20 minutes at room temperature, tossing again after 10 minutes.

Add the cheese and combine well. Cover and refrigerate the salad for several hours. Toss it again before serving cold or at room temperature.

Divide the salad among six plates and garnish each salad with six cherry tomato halves, cut side up, that have been sprinkled lightly with the remaining chopped parsley.
Serves 6

Mexican Bean Salad with Green Chili Dressing and Pan Corn Bread

*H*ere is my favorite version of layered Mexican bean salad. The green chili dressing adds just the right amount of "heat." Any number of ingredients such as crumbled bacon, chopped artichoke hearts, and thinly sliced celery can also be used in the recipe, so you can substitute favorites in equal amounts. The dense pan corn bread goes wonderfully well with the salad, but tortilla chips can be served too, or substituted. A large pitcher of white sangria or fresh limeade completes the meal. I prepare the salad and dressing several hours before serving it, cook the corn bread so that it can be served hot, and make the sangria or limeade last.

2½ cups shredded iceberg lettuce
1½ cups cooked drained and cooled kidney beans, or canned drained and rinsed kidney beans
2 cups cooked drained and cooled fresh or frozen corn kernels
2 cups diced tomato
2 cups cooked drained and cooled chick-peas, or canned drained and rinsed chick-peas
1 cup diced cored and seeded green bell pepper
½ cup diced red onion
2 cups cooked drained and cooled chili beans, or canned drained and rinsed chili beans
2 avocados, peeled, pitted, and cut into ½-inch cubes
1 lemon, halved and seeded
1½ cups sour cream
1½ cups shredded Monterey Jack cheese
1 recipe Pan Corn Bread (page 17)

Green Chili Dressing:

1 jalapeño pepper, seeded and finely chopped (optional)
2 tablespoons chopped fresh cilantro (coriander)
2 tablespoons chopped fresh parsley
⅓ cup white wine vinegar
1 cup virgin olive oil
1 teaspoon chili powder
Few dashes hot sauce
½ teaspoon ground cumin
½ cup finely chopped canned green chilis
1 teaspoon minced garlic

In a large 6- to 8-quart bowl with as straight or vertical sides as possible, arrange layers of each salad ingredient beginning with the lettuce, in the order listed, through the avocado.

Squeeze the lemon halves over the avocados. Cover the salad and refrigerate until ready to serve.

Make the dressing by combining all the ingredients in a medium-sized bowl and mixing well. Cover and refrigerate until needed. The salad will keep for several hours.

Just before serving the salad, pour the mixed dressing over the top slowly and evenly.

Serve the salad accompanied by bowls of sour cream and cheese and hot corn bread and butter.

Serves 6

Pan Corn Bread

1½ cups yellow cornmeal
1 cup all-purpose flour
2 teaspoons baking powder
1 tablespoon sugar
1 teaspoon salt
2 large eggs, lightly beaten
5 tablespoons melted butter (reserve
   1 tablespoon for the pan)

¾ cup sour cream
1 cup canned cream-style corn
¼ cup milk
½ cup grated Cheddar cheese
1 tablespoon peanut or vegetable oil

Preheat the oven to 400°.

Combine the cornmeal, flour, baking powder, sugar, and salt in a large bowl.

In another large bowl mix together all the remaining ingredients except for the oil and the fifth tablespoon melted butter, and pour over the dry ingredients. Combine well.

Brush the oil and the reserved tablespoon of melted butter over the bottom and sides of a heavy 10-inch iron skillet and heat the pan in the oven for 5 minutes.

Turn the batter into the hot pan and bake for about 25 minutes, or until done (a cake tester will come out clean).

Cool the corn bread 10 minutes before cutting into wedges and serving.

Makes 10 to 12 wedges

Black Bean and Crunchy Vegetable Salad

*T*his uncommonly delicious black bean salad is accompanied by fried flour tortilla wedges. Spread these crisp crackers with guacamole (page 186) and/or add grilled sweet Italian sausages if desired.

For a Spanish accent, add 1 teaspoon each of chili powder and cumin to the dressing.

> 3 cups cooked drained and cooled black beans
>   or canned drained and rinsed black beans
> ½ cup diced peeled carrot
> ½ cup diced cored and seeded red bell pepper
> ½ cup thinly sliced canned water chestnuts
> 8 crisp cooked bacon strips, crumbled
>   (optional)
> ½ cup chopped cauliflower
> 3 thinly sliced scallions
> 2 tablespoons chopped fresh parsley
> 8 large green cabbage leaves
> 1 recipe Fried Flour Tortilla Wedges

Basic Vinaigrette with Garlic:

> 1 garlic clove, minced
> ¼ cup red wine vinegar
> Salt and freshly ground pepper to taste
> ¾ cup virgin olive oil

In a large bowl combine the beans with the other salad ingredients through the parsley.

Make the dressing by whisking together the garlic, vinegar, and salt and pepper with a wire whisk in a small bowl, then drop by drop whisking in the olive oil.

Pour the dressing over the salad and toss. Let rest for 15 minutes. Toss the salad again and taste for salt and pepper.

Line each of four dinner plates with two cabbage leaves, spoon equal amounts of the salad over the cabbage, and serve with the fried tortilla wedges.

NOTE: This salad can be made a day in advance and kept covered in the refrigerator. If using the bacon, don't add it until just before the final mixing of the dish before serving so that it will remain crisp. The tortillas must be cooked right before serving.

Serves 4

Fried Flour Tortilla Wedges

> 4 8-inch flour tortillas
> ¾ cup vegetable oil

Cut the tortillas into six wedges each. Heat the vegetable oil in a large frying pan and cook the tortilla wedges on each side until golden and crisp. This will only take a few seconds.

Drain on paper towels and serve warm or at room temperature.

Makes 24 small wedges

Marinated Bean Salad in Roast Beef Packages

*H*ere is a hearty main course salad that I like to serve on special occasions in winter after a first course of French onion soup.

- 2 *cups cooked drained and cooled kidney beans, or canned drained and rinsed kidney beans (¾ cup dried beans)*
- 1 *10-ounce package frozen baby lima beans, cooked, drained, and cooled*
- ½ *cup thinly sliced celery hearts*
- ¼ *cup diced pimiento*
- 1 *pound thinly sliced roast beef*
- 4 *¼-inch-thick tomato slices*
- 1 *bunch watercress, washed, dried, and stem ends trimmed*
- 2 *teaspoons chopped fresh parsley*

Green Peppercorn Dressing I:

- 2 *tablespoons red wine vinegar*
- 1 *tablespoon Dijon mustard*
- 1 *egg yolk, at room temperature*
- 1 *teaspoon drained and coarsely chopped green peppercorns packed in brine*
- ¾ *cup olive oil*
- *Salt and freshly ground pepper to taste*

Combine the beans, celery hearts, and pimientos in a large bowl.

To make the dressing, whisk together the vinegar, mustard, egg yolk, and peppercorns in a small bowl; drop by drop whisk in the oil, then season with salt and pepper.

Pour the dressing over the bean mixture, cover, and refrigerate for several hours.

Cover each of four dinner plates with overlapping slices of roast beef in equal amounts. With a slotted spoon to allow any extra dressing to drip back into the bowl instead of onto the beef, put equal portions of the bean mixture onto the center of each plate. Fold the sides of the beef up over the salads on each plate, carefully turn each "package" over, and top with a tomato slice.

Surround each roast beef package with sprigs of watercress, spoon a little of the extra dressing over the watercress and tomato slices, sprinkle the parsley over the tomatoes, and serve.

Serves 4

Minestrone Salad with Tomato Vinaigrette

The salad version of the hearty Italian soup, minestrone, provides an equally hearty meal-in-one-dish salad with little fuss and lots of flavor. The recipe can be made a day ahead. Toasted sesame seed breadsticks and sweet butter are a good accompaniment.

1 cup cooked ditali or small macaroni (½ cup dried), drained and tossed in 1 tablespoon olive oil
1 cup diced boiled and drained potatoes
1 cup cooked green beans, cut into 1-inch lengths
1 cup canned drained and rinsed chick-peas
1 cup canned drained and rinsed red kidney beans
½ cup diced raw unpeeled zucchini
1 young leek, carefully washed and diced (white part only)
1 cup diced seeded tomato
2 cups finely shredded green cabbage
3 tablespoons chopped fresh basil
2 tablespoons chopped fresh Italian (flat-leaf) parsley

Tomato Vinaigrette:
6 tablespoons red wine vinegar
1 teaspoon Dijon mustard
½ teaspoon sugar
1 large garlic clove, minced
¾ cup olive oil
¾ cup tomato sauce
Salt and freshly ground pepper to taste

Combine all the salad ingredients in a large bowl.

To make the vinaigrette, whisk together the vinegar, mustard, sugar, and garlic in a medium bowl; drop by drop whisk in the oil and tomato sauce, then season to taste with salt and pepper.

Turn the dressing over the salad and toss. Cover and chill for several hours. Retoss before serving.

Serves 4

Molded Curried Couscous and Shrimp Salad

Couscous is a Moroccan grain made from semolina wheat. Quick-cooking couscous makes superb salads, served warm or cold. This particular salad combines couscous with shrimp, vegetables, raisins, and crunchy toasted almonds. I serve it with a mixed green salad, toasted pita bread wedges, and iced tea or lemonade with sprigs of fresh mint.

The recipe is easily doubled to serve eight, and the shrimp can be eliminated if desired.

3 tablespoons butter
½ cup almond slivers
1½ cups homemade or canned chicken broth
1 cup quick-cooking couscous
1 tablespoon curry powder
¼ teaspoon ground cinnamon
1 pound cooked shelled and deveined small
   shrimp
2 large carrots, peeled, diced, and blanched
¾ cup cooked and drained fresh or frozen corn
   kernels
¾ cup cooked and drained fresh or frozen
   green peas
½ cup raisins
2 scallions, thinly sliced
1 tablespoon fresh grated orange rind
Vegetable oil to brush dish
1 orange, cut into ⅛-inch-thick slices, then
   slices cut in half

Melt 1 tablespoon of the butter in a medium saucepan. Add the almonds and cook over medium heat, stirring constantly, until lightly browned. Drain on paper towels.

Bring the chicken broth to a boil in a medium saucepan. Stir in the remaining 2 tablespoons of butter and the couscous, curry, and cinnamon. Cover, remove from the heat, and let rest for 5 minutes.

Transfer the couscous to a large bowl; add the almonds and shrimp and remaining ingredients through the grated orange rind. Combine well.

Brush a 5-cup mold or soufflé dish lightly with oil. Spoon the mixture into the dish and lightly press it down, evenly. Wait 10 minutes to unmold it, or cover it and refrigerate until ready to serve.

To unmold the dish, place a plate or platter over the couscous; carefully holding onto each, invert the dish, shake once, and lift off the mold.

Garnish the salad with the orange slices and serve at room temperature or cold.

Serves 4

Lentil and Vegetable Salad with Spedini

This hearty salad of fragrant, vegetable-laced, plump lentils, served warm, is particularly pleasant fall or winter fare. Spedini—broiled bread and cheese kebabs—provide an unusual accompaniment.

1 cup lentils (no-soak type) rinsed, picked over, and drained
1 medium-sized yellow onion, minced
1 garlic clove, minced
1 cup diced carrot
1 cup diced celery
Salt and freshly ground pepper to taste
1 cup diced peeled and seeded tomato
½ cup diced cauliflower
¼ cup chopped shallot
2 tablespoons chopped fresh parsley
1 tablespoon finely chopped fresh basil, or
    1 teaspoon dried basil
4 tablespoons red wine vinegar or to taste
1 tablespoon Dijon mustard
½ cup olive oil
1 recipe Spedini

Cover the lentils, onion, garlic, carrots, and celery with 1 inch of water in a saucepan, and bring to a boil. Reduce the heat and simmer for about 30 minutes, or until the lentils are tender. Drain.

Combine the lentils and the remaining salad ingredients in a large bowl.

Combine the dressing ingredients in a small bowl, pour over the salad, and toss.

Serve the salad warm, with the Spedini.

Serves 4

Spedini

20 1-inch-thick slices ficelle (small French baguettes)
16 ½-inch-thick slices mozzarella, approximately the same size as the bread
Olive oil

Thread alternating slices of the bread and cheese on each of four 8-inch dampened wooden skewers, beginning and ending with a slice of the bread. Brush each kebab lightly with olive oil. Broil them on a rack in a pan over a baking sheet for about 2 minutes on each side, until the bread is lightly toasted. Serve immediately.

Tabouli with Minced Lamb

*T*abouli, the fine Middle Eastern salad, is a combination of bulgur wheat, finely minced mint and parsley, vegetables, lemon juice, and olive oil. It's an extremely popular salad in America today because it's healthy, hearty, and deliciously different. I've added a few extra minced vegetables and cooked lamb, which make the salad more substantial, and the lamb flavor certainly enhances the dish. Vegetarians can eliminate the lamb and substitute 1 cup of cooked dried or canned drained black, kidney, pinto, or other cooked beans.

Serve the salad with toasted pita bread, if desired.

1 cup bulgur wheat (not *instant tabouli*)
½ cup chopped fresh mint
½ cup chopped fresh parsley
¼ cup thinly sliced scallion
1 cup chopped seeded tomato
½ cup diced celery
½ cup diced cucumber (seeds scraped away)
1 cup minced cooked and drained lamb
Juice of 1 lemon or to taste
½ cup olive oil or as needed
Salt and freshly ground pepper to taste

1 small head romaine lettuce, washed, dried, and torn into bite-sized pieces

Put the bulgur wheat into a large bowl, cover it with water 1 inch over its surface, and soak for 30 minutes. Drain the wheat in a fine sieve or colander; then put into a clean dish cloth and press slightly to extract any extra water.

Put the bulgur wheat into a large bowl, add the remaining ingredients except for the romaine lettuce, and toss lightly, combining well. Taste for seasoning. The salad should be moist and lemony, but not wet. Add a little extra lemon juice and oil if needed.

Refrigerate the salad, covered, for at least 1 hour; 3 or 4 hours will bring out a fuller flavor.

Line a shallow serving dish with the lettuce, top with the salad, and serve cold.

NOTE: The salad can also be made the day before and kept covered in the refrigerator.

Serves 4

Quinoa and Sesame Shrimp Salad

Quinoa, a chock-full-of-protein grain, is available in specialty food shops.* A delicate grain, quinoa, when cooked, has the appearance of puffed transparent tiny beads, each with a tiny white germ ring. It has a most pleasing, light, slightly chewy texture with an earthy, nutty flavor, and is a great addition to salads and other dishes.

Serve with cucumber and whole wheat finger sandwiches spread lightly with sweet butter.

1 cup quinoa
Salt
¾ pound cooked shelled and deveined shrimp drained and chopped
¼ cup thinly sliced scallion
¼ cup minced canned water chestnuts
1 cup blanched snow pea pods, stemmed and stringed before blanching, cut into julienne strips lengthwise

Sesame Vinaigrette:

2 tablespoons red wine vinegar

* A Boulder, Colorado, company, the Quinoa Corporation, is packaging the product under the brand name Ancient Harvest.

1 tablespoon freshly squeezed lemon juice
2 tablespoons Oriental sesame oil or to taste
2 tablespoons safflower oil
Salt and freshly ground pepper to taste

Cook the quinoa covered with 1 inch of lightly salted water for about 15 minutes, or until tiny white germ rings appear. Drain well.

Combine the quinoa with the shrimp, scallions, water chestnuts, and snow pea pods.

Mix together the dressing ingredients in a small bowl, pour over the salad, and toss.

Serve immediately, or cover and chill well and serve cold.

Serves 4

Wheat Berry Mediterranean Salad

The crunchy texture and nutty flavor of wheat berries remind me of a combination of brown and wild rice. Wheat berries are an excellent base for salad-making and are available in health food shops.

This vegetarian salad, accented with

garlic, eggplant, and escarole that is sautéed in olive oil with sliced green olives, grated carrots, and zucchini, is finished with a fruity olive oil dressing. Serve with pumpernickel bread spread with sweet butter sprinkled with black pepper.

2 cups homemade chicken stock or canned chicken broth
4 cups water
2 cups wheat berries
¼ cup olive oil
1 teaspoon minced garlic
1 cup diced unpeeled eggplant
2 cups coarsely chopped washed and dried escarole
½ cup sliced pimiento-stuffed olives
½ cup grated unpeeled carrot
½ cup grated unpeeled zucchini
Salt and freshly ground pepper to taste

Parsley Vinaigrette:

3 tablespoons red wine vinegar
2 tablespoons freshly squeezed lemon juice
½ teaspoon minced garlic
2 tablespoons fresh chopped parsley
⅔ cup extra-virgin olive oil
Salt and freshly ground pepper to taste

Bring the stock to a boil with the water in a large pot. Add the wheat berries, stir, and simmer for about 1 hour, until tender but still crunchy, stirring occasionally. Drain and cool.

Meanwhile, heat the olive oil in a large frying pan, add the garlic and eggplant, and cook for 5 minutes, stirring often.

Add the escarole and cook 5 minutes more, stirring frequently. Cool.

To make the dressing, whisk together the vinegar, lemon juice, garlic, and parsley in a medium bowl; drop by drop whisk in the oil, then season to taste with salt and pepper.

Put the wheat berries into a large bowl and add the eggplant mixture and the olives, carrots, and zucchini. Pour the dressing over the ingredients, combine well, and season to taste with salt and pepper.

Serve at room temperature or chilled. (Salad can be made several hours ahead of time.)

Serves 4

CHEESE AND EGG SALADS

The versatility and nutritional values of cheese and eggs make them excellent bases for main course salads.

All types of cheeses can be used in main course salads, from soft to hard, and eggs, nature's perfectly portioned protein, are always available and affordable.

Cheese and eggs can make great last-minute main course salads for the family or unexpected guests, because we always are likely to have at least one kind of cheese and/or eggs on hand.

An unusual main course egg salad that my husband and I enjoy tremendously is made with a fluffy three-egg omelet. Each omelet is split evenly down the center, lengthwise, and filled with Caesar Salad. The recipe, Caesar Salad Omelet, is included in this chapter.

Another salad we particularly like we call Accident Salad because I discovered it by accident. Part of a meal I was serving one evening consisted of cheese fondue, made with Gruyère, and a tossed green salad of spinach, romaine, and chicory in a tart vinaigrette dressing. The fondue was almost at the point of readiness and in need of tasting, but the French bread cubes for dipping had already been put on the table. I drizzled some of the cheese fondue over a small portion of the mixed salad and found the combination incredibly delicious. When I related the story to our dinner guests, we all sampled the combination and agreed that a delectable new salad had been born.

I have also spooned cheese fondue over salads of hot cooked tiny new potatoes, sliced cornichon pickles, and boiled onions, which, of course, is a take-off on raclette.

RECIPES

Fried Mozzarella with Arugula, Red Onion, and Pine Nuts
Cheese Plateau Salads with French Walnut Bread
Gruyère, Celery, and Smoked Chicken Salad
Picasso Salad with Basil Beurre Blanc
Spinach Salad with Sun-Dried Tomatoes and Broiled Chèvre Medallions
Pasta and Three-Cheese Salad
Herb Omelet Salads with Smoked Salmon and Chive Sour Cream
Egg and Tuna Salad with Chutney
Caesar Salad Omelet
Deviled Egg and Corned Beef Salad
Presto Maria Salad

Fried Mozzarella with Arugula, Red Onion, and Pine Nuts

Recently, restaurants have been offering a fantastic creation of giant flattened, breaded, and fried veal cutlets topped with a mixed salad and pungent dressing. Liking the dish so much, but not the cost of veal, I adapted the recipe using fried mozzarella.

To complete a light meal, serve for dessert a scoop of raspberry sorbet in each of four balloon wine glasses, topped with blueberries.

1 pound mozzarella, cut into 8 ½-inch-thick slices
Flour
2 large eggs, lightly beaten
1 cup plain bread crumbs
3 tablespoons butter
½ cup pine nuts
¼ cup peanut or vegetable oil
1½ large bunches arugula, washed, dried, and stem ends trimmed
1 medium-sized red onion, diced
1 cup diced seeded tomato

Sherry Wine Vinaigrette:
2 tablespoons sherry wine vinegar
2 tablespoons red wine vinegar
1 tablespoon Dijon mustard
½ cup olive oil
Salt and freshly ground pepper to taste

Coat the cheese slices with flour, dip in the beaten eggs and coat evenly, then dredge in the bread crumbs, pressing slightly. Let the slices rest on a baking sheet.

Meanwhile, heat the butter in a large frying pan and cook the pine nuts for a few minutes until lightly browned, over medium heat, stirring often. Drain and set aside.

Add the oil to the butter in the frying pan and cook the breaded mozzarella in batches until golden brown, about 1 minute per side. Be sure to turn with a spatula.

Combine the arugula, onion, tomato, and pine nuts in a large bowl.

To make the dressing, whisk together the vinegars and mustard in a small bowl, drop by drop whisk in the olive oil, then season well to taste with salt and pepper. Pour the vinaigrette over the salad and toss.

Arrange the salad in equal portions across the center of each of four dinner plates. Put two slices of fried mozzarella on each plate, one on each side of the salad, and serve immediately.

Serves 4

Cheese Plateau Salads with French Walnut Bread

Aplateau of four different cheeses accompanied by crisp mixed greens and freshly baked walnut bread is nothing short of ambrosia. The combination is especially satisfying for cheese lovers and for vegetarians.

The bread can be made in advance and frozen, if time is a consideration.

The cheeses that I've selected can be substituted with another cheese of each particular type. For example: for the Gorgonzola, substitute Roquefort, bleu de Bress, or Danish blue, etc.; for l'Explorateur, substitute Brie or Pont l'Eveque, etc.; for Emmentaler, Gouda or Cheddar, etc.; for Montrachet, another goat cheese such as California chèvre.

Be sure to serve the cheeses at room temperature. Offer sweet butter and red wine if desired.

6 ounces Gorgonzola
6 ounces l'Explorateur
6 ounces Emmentaler
6 ounces Montrachet

1 cup each bite-sized pieces washed and dried Bibb lettuce, chicory, arugula, Boston lettuce, and red radicchio
1 recipe French Walnut Bread

Walnut Oil Vinaigrette:

4 tablespoons red wine vinegar
2 teaspoons Dijon mustard
2 tablespoons walnut oil
½ cup virgin olive oil
Salt and freshly ground pepper to taste

Cut each piece of cheese into four equal-sized pieces (1½ ounces each) and arrange one piece of each type in a "plateau" at the side of each of four large plates.

Combine the greens in a large bowl.

To make the dressing, whisk together the vinegar and mustard in a small bowl, drop by drop whisk in the oils, then season to taste with salt and pepper.

Pour the dressing over the greens and toss.

Divide the salad evenly among the four plates and serve with slices of walnut bread.
Serves 4

French Walnut Bread

Prepare the walnut bread several hours before serving so it can cool, or make it in advance and freeze it. (Thaw at room temperature for 2 hours, if frozen, and warm in oven.)

1½ cups whole wheat flour
2 cups all-purpose flour
1¼ cups chopped walnuts
1 package plus 1 teaspoon RapidRise yeast
1 teaspoon salt
1 cup water
⅓ cup milk
1 tablespoon molasses
Flour
⅓ cup raisins (optional)
Walnut oil

Combine the flours, ¾ cup of the walnuts, the yeast, and the salt in the container of a food processor.

Heat the water, milk, and molasses in a small pan to 115° to 120°.

Through the feed tube of the food processor, with the machine running, add the hot liquid. Run the machine until the dough forms a ball and falls off the side of the container.

Transfer the dough to a lightly floured countertop or cutting board and knead in the remaining walnuts and the raisins.

Put the dough into a large, lightly oiled bowl, cover with a cloth, and let the dough rise in a warm, draft-free spot for 45 minutes, or until it has doubled in size.

Push the dough down, shape it into one long or round loaf, and put it on a baking sheet. Make several shallow diagonal slashes in the surface of the dough with a very sharp knife. Let rise about 20 minutes, covered with the cloth.

Meanwhile, preheat the oven to 400°.

Remove the cloth and bake the bread for 45 minutes.

Cool the bread on a baking rack at least 30 minutes before slicing.

Makes 1 loaf

Gruyère, Celery, and Smoked Chicken Salad

Accompany this refreshing salad with toasted French bread and sweet butter.

1 pound smoked chicken breasts, skinned and thinly sliced
1½ cups shredded Gruyère cheese
1½ cups thinly sliced celery, cut on the diagonal
8 cherry tomatoes
8 large black olives

Shallot Dressing:

1 teaspoon Dijon mustard
1 tablespoon freshly squeezed lemon juice
2 tablespoons white wine vinegar
1 shallot, minced
⅔ cup virgin olive oil
1 tablespoon chopped fresh parsley
Salt and freshly ground pepper to taste

Arrange the smoked chicken over the bottom of four dinner plates in equal amounts.

In a large bowl combine the cheese and celery.

To make the dressing, whisk together the mustard, lemon juice, vinegar, and shallot in a medium bowl; drop by drop whisk in the oil; add the parsley; then season to taste with salt and pepper.

Add the dressing to the combined cheese and celery, and toss.

Spoon the mixture over the chicken on each plate in equal amounts, garnish each salad with two cherry tomatoes and two black olives, and serve.

Serves 4

Picasso Salad with Basil Beurre Blanc

This appetizing salad is a mélange of colors, flavors, and textures. Fresh vegetables are barely cooked, then combined and crowned with a poached egg. The fresh Basil Beurre Blanc blankets the ingredients, resulting in an irresistible combination.

Salt
3 cups water
8 asparagus spears, ends trimmed, stems peeled, and cut on the diagonal into ½-inch pieces
1 cup chopped broccoli stalks
3 medium-sized carrots, peeled and cut into julienne strips

1 medium unpeeled zucchini, cut into julienne
strips
½ cup diced celery
½ cup diced cored and seeded yellow or red
bell pepper
2 teaspoons white vinegar
4 large eggs, at room temperature

Basil Beurre Blanc:

1 tablespoon minced shallot
¼ cup red wine vinegar
2 sticks butter (½ pound)
¼ cup finely sliced fresh basil
Salt and freshly ground pepper to taste

Lightly salt the water, bring it to a boil, and cook the asparagus, broccoli, carrots, zucchini, and celery for 3 minutes. Drain the vegetables well, put into a large bowl with the pepper, and combine.

Put 1 inch of water in a large frying pan and bring to a boil for poaching the eggs.

Meanwhile, prepare the beurre blanc: Boil the shallots and vinegar until the vinegar is reduced to 1 tablespoon, over low heat. Whisk in the butter, a tablespoon at a time. The sauce should thicken. Stir in the basil and season to taste with salt and pepper. Remove from the heat and cover to keep warm.

Then poach the eggs as follows: When the water is boiling, add the vinegar and lower the heat to a simmer. Break each egg into a saucer and carefully slide into the simmering water in different areas of the pan so that the eggs do not touch each other. Spoon hot water from the pan over each of the eggs for a few seconds. Cook the eggs until the whites are set but the yolk remains runny—about 4 minutes.

While the eggs are poaching, divide the vegetables in equal portions among four large soup plates.

With a slotted spoon, remove each egg, gently turn each over onto a doubled piece of paper towel to drain it, then put one egg on top of each salad.

Spoon equal amounts of the warm beurre blanc over the salads and serve immediately.
Serves 4

Spinach Salad with Sun-Dried Tomatoes and Broiled Chèvre Medallions

Spinach salad consisting of young spinach leaves, mushrooms, red onion rings, and bacon with a fragrant vinaigrette dressing is a fine main course salad, not quite dated, especially for those who love it. The addition of sun-dried tomatoes and broiled goat cheese on French bread reflects current tastes and enhances the salad tremendously.

1 quart young spinach leaves, washed, dried, and stem ends trimmed
10 ounces fresh mushrooms, thinly sliced
1 medium-sized red onion, thinly sliced, rings separated
12 strips crisp cooked bacon, crumbled
8 sun-dried tomatoes in olive oil, cut into thin strips
1 recipe Broiled Chèvre Medallions

Herb Vinaigrette:

1 tablespoon Dijon mustard
1 egg yolk, at room temperature
1 garlic clove, minced
4 tablespoons red wine vinegar
⅔ cup extra-virgin olive oil
Salt and freshly ground pepper to taste

First make the vinaigrette: Whisk together the mustard, egg yolk, garlic, and vinegar in a medium bowl. Drop by drop whisk in the oil, then season to taste with salt and pepper. Set aside.

Put the spinach leaves in a large bowl and top with the mushrooms, onion rings, bacon, and sun-dried tomatoes.

Whisk the dressing again, pour it over the salad, and toss well.

Put equal portions of the salad on four dinner plates, garnish each with three broiled chèvre medallions, and serve immediately.
Serves 4

Broiled Chèvre Medallions

12 ¼-inch-thick slices French bread
Virgin olive oil
8 ounces Montrachet goat cheese log, cut crosswise into 12 equal-sized medallions

Brush the bread slices lightly with olive oil, put on a baking sheet, and lightly toast under the broiler.

Top each slice of toasted bread with a

medallion of cheese and drizzle a little olive oil over each. Pass under the broiler again until golden brown, only a minute or two.

Makes 12 medallions

Pasta and Three-Cheese Salad

Serve this lovely pasta tossed salad with a side dish of mixed greens in the dressing of your choice, crusty Italian bread, and a chilled bottle of dry Italian wine, such as Pinot Grigio.

3 quarts water
8 ounces dry penne or ziti
1 tablespoon salt
¾ cup diced Fontina cheese
¾ cup diced Swiss cheese
½ cup shredded Parmesan cheese
2 tablespoons chopped fresh basil, or
   1 teaspoon dried basil
1 teaspoon chopped fresh thyme, or ½ teaspoon
   dried thyme
1 cup diced seeded tomato
2 tablespoons chopped fresh Italian (flat-leaf)
   parsley

Sour Cream Dressing I:

1 tablespoon grated yellow onion
4 tablespoons red wine vinegar
¾ cup olive oil
¼ cup sour cream
Salt and freshly ground pepper to taste

Bring the water to a boil in a large pot. Add the salt, stir, add the penne, and stir again. Cook the pasta *al dente*, or just until tender, about 8 minutes, stirring often.

To make the dressing, whisk together the onion and vinegar in a medium bowl, drop by drop whisk in the oil, then whisk in the sour cream and season well to taste with salt and pepper.

Drain the pasta well and transfer to a large bowl. Pour the dressing over the warm pasta and toss. Let cool for 15 minutes.

Add the remaining ingredients, combine well, and serve hot or at room temperature.

Serves 4

Herb Omelet Salads with Smoked Salmon and Chive Sour Cream

*H*ere is an unusual salad of today—a lovely composed egg salad made of individual herb-filled omelets sliced into medallions and coupled with slices of smoked salmon. A drizzle of chive, cream, and lemon-laced sour cream zigzags flavor across the top. Please note: Only fresh herbs can be used in the recipe.

Accompany with French bread and sweet butter, if desired.

1 tablespoon chopped fresh parsley
1 tablespoon chopped fresh tarragon
1 tablespoon chopped fresh dill
1 tablespoon chopped fresh basil
12 large eggs, at room temperature
Salt and freshly ground pepper
4 tablespoons butter
4 tablespoons heavy cream
12 thin slices smoked salmon

Chive Sour Cream:

¾ cup sour cream
1 tablespoon freshly squeezed lemon juice
3 tablespoons heavy cream
2 tablespoons freshly snipped chives
Salt and freshly ground pepper to taste

Combine the parsley, tarragon, dill, and basil in a small bowl and prepare the four omelets individually in the following manner.

Whisk together 3 of the eggs and season with salt and pepper. Heat 1 tablespoon of the butter in an 8-inch nonstick or seasoned omelet pan or a frying pan with curved sides. Swirl the butter around in the pan and add the eggs. Immediately stir them in a circle with a fork, and cook over medium heat until the eggs just begin to set. Quickly stir in 1 tablespoon of the heavy cream, and spread the egg mixture evenly over the bottom of the pan.

Sprinkle 1 tablespoon of the combined herbs down the center of the eggs. Tilt the pan slightly and, with a tablespoon, turn the solidified eggs over the herbs, little by little, until an omelet roll is formed. Turn the omelet out onto a plate.

Repeat for the three remaining omelets.

Combine the chive-sour cream dressing ingredients in a small bowl and taste for seasoning.

Arrange three slices of the smoked salmon across one side of each of four large plates. Slice each omelet into ¼-inch-thick medallions and arrange in rows next to the salmon on each plate.

Drizzle the dressing over the omelets and salmon in a crisscross pattern in equal amounts and serve immediately.

Serves 4

Egg and Tuna Salad with Chutney

This creamy, flavorful salad is a delightful extension of basic egg salad. I always serve it with toasted white bread, generously buttered and cut into toast points, and ice cold milk or iced tea.

For a delicious variation, substitute flaked boneless and skinless sardines or smoked trout for the tuna.

6 hard-boiled eggs, coarsely chopped
1 6½-ounce can solid white-meat tuna, drained and flaked
¼ cup diced cored and seeded yellow bell pepper
¼ cup minced sweet gherkin pickles
1 teaspoon celery seeds
½ cup diced mango chutney
¾ cup mayonnaise or Classic Mayonnaise (page 128)

Salt and freshly ground pepper to taste
3 cups romaine lettuce leaves, washed, dried, and torn into bite-sized pieces
1 tablespoon chopped fresh parsley

Combine the eggs, tuna, pepper, pickles, and celery seeds in a large bowl.

Mix together the chutney and mayonnaise, turn over the salad, combine well, and season to taste with salt and pepper.

Spoon into a serving dish and surround with the lettuce. Sprinkle with the parsley and serve.

Serves 4

Caesar Salad Omelet

My husband and I enjoy a light summer meal of fluffy three-egg omelets split evenly down the center and filled with Caesar salad. (The usual one-minute cooked egg is eliminated from the Caesar salad.) Warm French bread, sweet butter, and chilled white wine go very well with this omelet salad. For dessert, serve Nutmeg Ice Cream,* alone or with fresh berries or sliced peaches or bananas.

3 tablespoons vegetable oil
2 ½-inch-thick slices French bread, cut into ½-inch cubes
2 cups shredded romaine lettuce
2 tablespoons freshly grated Parmesan cheese, or to taste
6 large eggs, at room temperature
Salt and freshly ground pepper
4 teaspoons sweet butter

Anchovy Dressing I:

2 anchovy fillets, drained and minced
1 small garlic clove, peeled and minced
1 tablespoon fresh lemon juice
⅓ cup virgin olive oil
½ teaspoon Worcestershire sauce
Salt and freshly ground pepper to taste

First, heat the oil in a skillet and lightly brown the bread cubes all over. Drain on paper towels.

Then make the dressing: Combine the anchovies, garlic, and lemon juice in a small bowl; drop by drop, whisk in the olive oil; add the Worcestershire sauce, then season to taste with salt and pepper.

Make each omelet individually as follows: Whip three eggs lightly together and season to taste with salt and pepper. Melt 2 teaspoons of the butter in a 9-inch nonstick or seasoned omelet pan or frying pan with curved sides, and add the eggs. Stir in a circle with a fork until the eggs begin to set. Smooth them over with the back of a spoon and tilt one end of the pan. Fold the eggs over and turn out onto a plate. Immediately slit the omelet down the center, about one inch from each end, and spread apart.

Prepare the second omelet.

Toss the lettuce, croutons, Parmesan cheese, and dressing together, spoon into the center of each of the omelets equally, and serve immediately.
Serves 2

* To prepare Nutmeg Ice Cream: Several hours in advance, soften 1 pint of good-quality vanilla ice cream and stir in ⅛ teaspoon of fresh grated nutmeg. Refreeze.

Deviled Egg and Corned Beef Salad

*T*he harmony of eggs combined with corned beef in this easy salad produces an excellent dish that has become a favorite fall and winter meal in my family. Serve with toasted seeded rye bread and sweet butter and, for a special treat, French fried potatoes.

    5 hard-boiled large eggs, coarsely chopped
    2 cups cubed leftover or delicatessen corned beef
    ¾ cup mayonnaise or Classic Mayonnaise
       (page 128)
    2 tablespoons red wine vinegar
    1 tablespoon Dijon mustard
    3 tablespoons minced cornichon pickles
    Salt and freshly ground pepper
    1 teaspoon paprika
    4 romaine lettuce leaves

Combine the eggs and corned beef in a large bowl.

Mix together the remaining ingredients except the paprika in a small bowl, turn over the eggs and corned beef, and combine well.

Sprinkle with the paprika and serve, or cover and chill well. Serve in equal portions on lettuce leaves.

Serves 4

Presto Maria Salad

*I*n Italian *presto* means "hurry up," which expresses exactly how easily and quickly this delicious salad, which combines pure natural foods and flavors, can be made. Serve with breadsticks for a light meal-in-one dish.

    ¾ pound mozzarella, cut into ¼-inch-thick
       sticks, about 1 inch in length
    1 pint cherry tomatoes, halved
    ½ pound sliced mortadella, cut into julienne
       strips
    1 small red onion, thinly sliced
    12 leaves fresh basil, thinly sliced
    Salt and freshly ground pepper to taste
    Virgin olive oil
    White wine vinegar

Combine the cheese, tomatoes, mortadella, red onion, and basil in a large bowl.

Sprinkle with salt and pepper, a little olive oil, and vinegar to taste, toss, and serve.

Serves 4

FRUIT SALADS

One of the most beautiful fruit salads that I've ever encountered was served to a dieting friend at The Four Seasons restaurant in New York City. He'd requested plain boiled shrimp with a little fruit salad for his main course, while the rest of our party ordered elaborate dishes from the restaurant's extensive menu.

When our dinners were placed simultaneously in front of us, everyone's attention was drawn to our friend's special order. At the center of a large white plate stood a pyramid of plump pink shrimp, surrounded by thinly sliced fans of papaya, mango, kiwi fruit, peach, pear, banana, apple, and huge strawberries, punctuated by raspberries and grapefruit sections. As good as our dishes proved to be, we were all a little envious of our companion's simple shrimp and fruit salad, so magnificently presented.

There really is nothing quite as refreshing as a fruit salad composed of perfect, ripe, seasonal fresh fruit. A fruit salad can qualify as a main course for a light meal with enough quantity to satisfy the diner; the meal can also include croissants, brioche, banana bread, French rolls, muffins, or crackers. Or fruit salads can be made more substantial with the addition of cheeses, seafood, and meat, as you will see in the following recipes.

Healthful main course fruit salads can be plain or a bit exotic. Slivered breast of chicken and pecans with fresh blueberries combined with sweetened mayonnaise highlighted with a dash of lemon juice and vanilla essence and garnished with a border of honeydew melon balls, for example, or alternating slices of cantaloupe, Black Forest ham, and Brie with a diced mustard fruit or chutney sweet-and-sour dressing come to mind as interesting possibilities for main course fruit salads. Put your creative talents and instincts to work using favorite fruits and other complementing ingredients and dressings.

Fresh fruit is always best for a salad. I have never found a canned fruit in which the quality, texture, and flavor haven't suffered considerably during the canning process. And as far as I'm concerned, frozen fruits such as raspberries, strawberries, and blueberries are only good when pureed and used in mousses, ice creams, sorbets, butters, and sauces.

Sweetened dressings are natural fresh fruit salad enhancers. A honey-sweetened sour cream dressing with chopped dates and pomegranate might prove just the right dressing for certain fruit and meat, seafood, or cheese salads. Vinegar-and-oil-based dressings with herbs can be sweetened and spirited by the addition of honey, sugar, or sweet liqueurs, such as Grand Marnier, Crème de Menthe, or Amaretto, producing unexpectedly delicious dressings for fruit salads.

When creating your own variations, consider cutting the fruit into various contrasting shapes: cubes, wedges, slices, fingers, or balls. A mixed fruit salad of melon balls and blueberries in the center of a dish can be deliciously and attractively garnished with peeled sections of orange, grapefruit, and/or tangerine. Thinly sliced ham or prosciutto wrapped around pineapple or melon sticks or buttered breadsticks highlight a fruit salad that contains no other meat or seafood or the fruits mentioned.

Fruit butters go very well with main course fruit salads on breads or muffins. Puree about a half cup of fresh or frozen thawed and well-drained raspberries or strawberries, combine with 1 stick of softened butter along with 1 tablespoon of confectioner's sugar thoroughly and chill in a small bowl.

RECIPES

Fruit Salad with Yogurt, Granola, Almonds, and Coconut
Melon, Berry, and Fig Salad in Prosciutto with Toasted Pound Cake
Honeydew Melon with Fruit and Cheese and Raspberry Mayonnaise
Fruit Salad with Cinnamon Cream and Puff Pastry Crackers
Pineapples Stuffed with Tropical Fruit and Lobster Salad

Fruit Salad with Yogurt, Granola, Almonds, and Coconut

When I get a craving for something sweet, refreshing, and relatively low in calories, I am always totally satisfied with this eye-appealing composed salad. Serve it with bran muffins and sweet butter.

2 tablespoons butter
½ cup almond slivers
½ cup shredded coconut
1 small cantaloupe, halved, peeled, seeded, and cut into ¼-inch-thick slices
1 small fresh pineapple, skinned, cored, and cut into ½-inch-thick slices
1 papaya, halved, peeled, seeded, and cut into ¼-inch-thick slices (2 fresh peaches can be substituted)
1 pint fresh strawberries, hulled
2 bananas, peeled and cut into ¼-inch-thick slices on the diagonal
Bouquet of mint sprigs
1 cup vanilla yogurt
½ cup granola

Heat the butter in a medium-sized frying pan and cook the almond slivers until golden brown, stirring often. Drain on paper towels and set aside.

Spread the coconut on a baking sheet and put under the broiler. Stir frequently until golden brown. Watch carefully: coconut burns quickly because of its sugar content. Cool, stirring a few times to prevent the coconut from sticking together.

On a large serving platter arrange the fruit attractively in one layer. Garnish with the mint sprigs. Serve the fruit with the combined granola and yogurt, almonds, and coconut in separate bowls.
Serves 4

Melon, Berry, and Fig Salad in Prosciutto with Toasted Pound Cake

What an unusual presentation this lovely Italy-inspired salad makes. The colorful fruit is spooned onto a plate covered with prosciutto, then the ends of the prosciutto are brought up and turned over the fruit along the edges. Each salad is garnished with a fluted lime, and served with two round slices of toasted, buttered pound cake, which counteracts the lime-sprayed fruit and prosciutto beautifully.

The proportions in the recipe certainly constitute a main course salad, but cut in half the dish can act as a first course. While I particularly like this combination of fruit, other fresh fruit such as sliced strawberries, mangoes, papayas, bananas, peaches, pears, or orange sections can be substituted or added.

1 small cantaloupe, seeded and cut into small balls or bite-sized cubes
½ honeydew melon, seeded and cut into small balls or bite-sized cubes
1 pint fresh blueberries, stems removed
1 cup fresh raspberries (reserve 4 for garnishing the limes)
4 ripe figs, peeled and quartered
2 limes
1 pound thinly sliced prosciutto, at room temperature*
8 1-inch-thick slices pound cake, cut with a pastry cutter into 3-inch circles
2 tablespoons butter, softened

In a large bowl gently combine the fruit.
To make fluted lime halves, cut ¼ inch off of each lime at the stem end and the opposite end, and then cut the lime in half crosswise, in a zigzag fashion as follows: With a small sharp pointed knife, beginning at the center of each lime, insert the knife through the rind to the middle of the lime on an angle and cut a zigzag or W shape around the circumference. Separate the halves and remove the seeds.

Arrange the prosciutto slices in equal portions, slightly overlapping and hanging over the edges of each of four dinner plates by about 2 inches. Spoon equal portions of the fruit over the center of the prosciutto on each plate and fold the prosciutto up over the edges of the salad.

Garnish each plate with a fluted lime half standing on its flat-cut end with a raspberry in its center. (The lime is to be squeezed onto the salad.)

Spread the butter evenly over one side of each circle of pound cake and pass under the broiler until golden brown. Serve warm. Serve two slices with each salad.

Serves 4

* It is easier to separate prosciutto slices at room temperature; when cold they tend to stick together and tear.

Honeydew Melon with Fruit and Cheese and Raspberry Mayonnaise

*H*oneydew melon halves filled with fresh fruit tossed with mild-flavored cheeses and crowned with a raspberry-flavored mayonnaise provide cool substantial fare for a summer meal. Serve with toasted buttered whole wheat bread and ham finger sandwiches.

½ pint fresh strawberries, hulled
1 small cantaloupe, halved, seeded, and cut into small balls with a melon scoop
1 red Delicious apple, cored and thinly sliced
¼ pound Fontina cheese, cut into ½-inch cubes
¼ pound mild Cheddar cheese, cut into ½-inch cubes
¼ pound Halvarti, cut into ½-inch cubes
2 medium-sized honeydew melons, halved and seeded
¼ cup shelled green pumpkin seeds

Raspberry Mayonnaise:

½ cup mayonnaise, or Classic Mayonnaise (page 128)

½ cup pureed thawed frozen raspberries
1 teaspoon freshly squeezed lemon juice

Combine the fruits and cheeses in a large bowl and spoon equal amounts into the center of each melon half.

To make the raspberry mayonnaise, mix together the mayonnaise, raspberry puree, and lemon juice in a small bowl.

Top each salad with equal portions of the mayonnaise, sprinkle each with pumpkin seeds, and serve.
Serves 4

Fruit Salad with Cinnamon Cream and Puff Pastry Crackers

*B*efore retiring on a Saturday evening one weekend, I was challenged by my dieting family to prepare a Sunday brunch other than our usual favorite calorie-laden meals. I responded with the following layered fruit salad. Splurging on a few tablespoons of cream and two puff pastry crackers for each serving was deceiving, because each salad was less than five hundred calories. By comparison, a bacon, omelet, and croissant meal would have totaled well over a thousand calories each.

The puff pastry crackers can be served with any fruit salad or other salad.

4 kiwi fruit, peeled and thinly sliced
1 papaya, peeled, seeded, and thinly sliced
1 small cantaloupe, peeled, seeded, and thinly sliced
1 pint large fresh strawberries, hulled and thinly sliced
1 small honeydew melon, peeled, seeded, and thinly sliced
2 large navel oranges, peeled (including white pith), thinly sliced crosswise, and seeded
½ small pineapple, peeled, cored, and cut into thin slices
2 large fresh peaches, peeled, halved, pitted, and thinly sliced
2 ripe mangoes, peeled and cut into thin slices
1 cup heavy cream
¼ teaspoon ground cinnamon
2 tablespoons sugar
1 recipe Puff Pastry Crackers

Alternate slices of fruit, in the order that they are listed, on each of four dinner plates. Cover each plate with plastic wrap and refrigerate.

Combine the cream and cinnamon in a small saucepan, bring to a boil, and reduce to ¾ cup over high heat, whisking constantly. The cream will thicken. Stir the sugar into the cream and remove from the heat.

Immediately spoon about 3 tablespoons of the cream over each fruit salad and serve each salad with two puff pastry crackers.
Serves 4

Puff Pastry Crackers

1 sheet frozen puff pastry, thawed
Oil for greasing baking sheet

Preheat the oven to 400°.

Roll the sheet of puff pastry very thin and cut it into eight 3-inch circles with a pastry or cookie cutter.

Lightly grease a baking sheet and put the pastry circles on it, at least 1 inch apart. Bake for 10 minutes, then turn each piece with a spatula and cook another few minutes, until golden brown and crisp. Cool.
Makes 8 crackers

Pineapples Stuffed with Tropical Fruit and Lobster Salad

A salad stuffed in a fresh pineapple shell always is enticing and slightly exotic. This one, with ginger dressing and garnished with crunchy Chinese Fried Walnuts, is especially wonderful. The walnuts should be prepared first so they can cool.

There are two ways to stuff a pineapple. The easy way, described in this recipe, is to cut the pineapple in half lengthwise and hollow it out, with each pineapple serving two. In a more extravagant and expensive presentation, each diner is served a whole stuffed pineapple.*

2 medium-sized fresh pineapples
6 canned artichoke hearts, drained and quartered
2 ripe mangoes, peeled and diced
4 passion fruit, peeled and diced (if unavailable, use kiwi fruit)
4 canned hearts of palm, cut into ½-inch disks
2 cups chopped cooked lobster meat (page 181)
1 cup alfalfa sprouts
1 recipe Chinese Fried Walnuts (page 52)

Ginger Dressing:

1 teaspoon finely grated fresh ginger
1 tablespoon finely chopped shallot
2 tablespoons freshly squeezed lemon juice
2 tablespoons white wine vinegar
½ cup vegetable oil
½ cup pureed apricot preserves (puree in a blender or force through a sieve)
Salt and freshly ground pepper to taste

Cut each pineapple in half, cutting right through the leafy tops and stem ends. Cut away the core and pineapple fruit, leaving a ¾-inch pineapple shell and leaves intact. (A grapefruit knife is very helpful in accomplishing this procedure.)

Cut the edible pineapple into bite-sized pieces and put it into a bowl with the artichokes, fruit, hearts of palm, and lobster.

To make the dressing, whisk together the ginger, shallot, lemon juice, and vinegar; drop by drop whisk in the oil and then the pureed apricot preserves; then season to taste with salt and pepper.

Turn the dressing over the salad and toss.

Put each pineapple half on a large dinner plate and fill with equal portions of the salad.

Make four little nests out of the alfalfa sprouts, and place one beside each pineapple shell. Garnish the top of each salad with a few Chinese Fried Walnuts and put the remaining nuts in equal amounts into the center of the alfalfa sprout nests.

Serves 4

* *To stuff a whole pineapple,* cut 1½ inches off the top of the pineapple, then cut out the pineapple core and edible fruit, leaving a ¾-inch shell. Also cut about ¼ inch off the bottom of the pineapple, so that it will stand up on the plate steadily. Fill the shell with the salad and top with the leafy pineapple top.

Chinese Fried Walnuts

This crunchy garnish also serves as a great appetizer/hors d'oeuvre or food gift. I have given batches as Christmas and hostess gifts. (Double or triple all of the ingredients in the recipe.) In tightly covered jars they keep in the refrigerator for several weeks. Be sure to thoroughly cool the walnuts before storing them in jars.

½ cup sugar
½ cup water
1 cup walnut halves
2 cups peanut oil

Bring the sugar and water to a boil in a heavy-bottomed saucepan. Add the walnuts, stir, and cook for 1 minute. Drain in a colander in the sink.

Heat the peanut oil in a medium-sized frying pan and add the walnuts. Stir and cook over medium-high heat until golden brown.

Transfer the walnuts to a nonstick baking sheet and cool, separating with a spoon so that the walnuts don't stick together.

Makes 1 cup

MIXED GREEN SALADS

Mixed green salads are no longer as predictable as they used to be because of the broad spectrum of greens available in stores today.

In quality produce stalls, farmers' markets, and many supermarkets, the lettuce and greens displayed are beautiful still lifes of contrasting textures, colors, flavors, and shapes, among them the unique individual peppery taste of arugula and watercress, subtly flavored oakleaf, Bibb, and Boston lettuce, slightly bitter deep-rose-colored radicchio, and delicate endive or mache. Spinach, escarole, and chicory are more substantial greens and make fabulous main course salads.

Salads based on greens lend themselves to the addition of other ingredients such as croutons, potatoes, beans, nuts, vegetables, seafood, meat, or cheese. It is the added ingredients that give them main course status and nutritional balance.

One of my favorite main course green salads is Salade Frisée, a combination of chicory, crisp cooked bacon cubes, and croutons tossed in a warm tart dressing and topped with a poached egg for each serving. The recipe is included in this chapter.

The salads in this chapter represent only a few of the hundreds of possibilities for notable main course salads starring today's splendid greens. For vegetarians, any meat in the recipes can be replaced by cheese, nuts, grains, beans, or tofu.

Greens are always a great inspiration for creating new salad dressings. Blue cheese, hazelnut oil, and white wine vinegar vinaigrette as the dressing for a mixed green salad with strips of pork or lamb makes an exceptionally good main course salad, for instance. A raspberry vinegar dressing tossed with a combination of Bibb, Boston, and oakleaf lettuce with flattened sautéed chicken breast medallions is another interesting example.

The dressing needn't be exotic or made with expensive ingredients. A basic vinaigrette composed of top-quality vinegar and olive oil, a little salt and pepper, and perhaps a touch of mustard always makes a superb and simple dressing for greens.

RECIPES

Tossed Green Salad with Ham, Apples, Beets, and Walnuts
Salade Frisée
Romaine, Endive, and Arugula Caesar Salad with Sausage
Mixed Greens with Smoked Salmon
Mixed Greens with Fried Potato Scallops
Watercress and Romaine Salad with Sautéed Chicken Livers and Shallots
Arugula and Salami Salad with Parmesan Cheese

Tossed Green Salad with Ham, Apples, Beets, and Walnuts

*H*ere is an uncommonly good and colorful main course salad composed of complementing ingredients accented with Stilton cheese dressing. Roquefort or blue cheese can replace the Stilton cheese. I like to serve thick slices of fresh pumpernickel with sweet butter and ice cold beer or ale to finish the meal.

2 cups small bite-sized pieces washed and dried chicory
2 cups shredded washed and dried romaine lettuce
1 cup finely shredded red cabbage
½ pound boiled ham slices, cut into ¼-inch-thick strips
1 cup cubed unpeeled Granny Smith apple
1 cup cubed cooked beets
½ cup chopped walnuts
1 tablespoon chopped fresh parsley

Stilton Cheese Dressing:

3 tablespoons red wine vinegar
2 teaspoons minced shallot
1 egg yolk, at room temperature
1 teaspoon chopped fresh tarragon
   (½ teaspoon dried)
½ cup olive oil
½ cup crumbled Stilton cheese
¼ cup heavy cream
Salt and freshly ground pepper to taste

Combine the greens, cabbage, ham, apple, beets, and walnuts in a bowl.

To make the dressing: Whisk together the vinegar, shallots, and egg yolk. Drop by drop whisk in the oil. Stir in the cheese and cream, and season to taste with salt and pepper.

Turn the dressing over the salad, toss until well combined, and sprinkle with the parsley.

Serves 4

Salade Frisée

*I*n France, Salade Frisée, or Salade Lyonnaise, as it's known in Burgundy, is considered quite ordinary fare, and it can be found on hundreds of menus across the country every day. Yet I find that this salad is exceptional in its fine balance of flavors and textures.

Salade Frisée is a traditional salad in the

sense that at its base is a green, the frisée or chicory (curly endive). The dynamic flavors and textures of crisp bacon cubes, crunchy fresh-cooked croutons, and tart dressing, always a winning combination in a salad, are further enhanced by the addition of soothing, creamy poached eggs.

Because the dressing and poached eggs are warm when served, it's an especially nice salad on a fall or winter day. Salade Frisée is a perfect light lunch, Sunday brunch, or midnight dinner any season, though. Serve it with red wine and finish the meal with ripe pears and Brie.

For a variation for spring or summer, replace the eggs with diced roast chicken, sliced smoked turkey, or smoked salmon.

¾ pound slab bacon, cut into ½-inch cubes
2 medium-sized heads chicory, washed, well-dried, and torn into bite-sized pieces
2 teaspoons white vinegar
4 large eggs, at room temperature

Croutons:

½ cup olive oil
4 slices firm white bread, crusts trimmed off, cut into ½-inch cubes

Salade Frisée Dressing:

3 shallots, minced
⅓ cup white wine vinegar
½ cup olive oil
¼ cup vegetable oil
1 tablespoon bacon drippings
2 tablespoons Dijon mustard
Salt and freshly ground pepper to taste

Fry the bacon cubes in a large frying pan until crisp and golden, turning often. Drain the bacon on paper towels and set aside. Reserve 1 tablespoon of the bacon drippings for the dressing.

Then make the croutons. In a large, clean frying pan, heat the olive oil and fry the bread cubes until golden brown, stirring and turning them often. Drain on paper towels and set aside.

To make the dressing: Put the shallots, vinegar, oils, and bacon drippings in a small, heavy-bottomed saucepan and bring the mixture to a boil, whisking constantly. Immediately reduce the heat and simmer for 3 minutes. Remove from the heat, whisk in the mustard, and season well to taste with salt and pepper. Cover.

In a large, clean frying pan, bring 1½ inches of water to a boil for poaching the eggs.

Meanwhile put the chicory into a large salad bowl and add the cooked bacon cubes.

Then poach the eggs according to the directions on page 35.

While the eggs are poaching, whisk the dressing again, pour it over the greens and bacon, and toss. Add the croutons and toss again.

Divide the salad among four dinner plates in equal portions.

Then drain the eggs as directed on page 35, put one egg on top of each salad in the center, and serve immediately. Pass the peppermill.

Serves 4

Romaine, Endive, and Arugula Caesar Salad with Sausage

Clearly, a Caesar Salad is one of the world's great original salads, and the addition of Italian sausage provides enough protein for a main course, and an intriguing complementary flavor as well. Endive and arugula are included with the traditional romaine for a twist of today. Shrimp, chunks of canned white-meat tuna, or strips of broiled flank steak are all delectable alternatives to the sausage in the recipe.

4 sweet Italian sausages
1 medium head romaine lettuce, washed, dried, and torn into bite-sized pieces
2 Belgian endive, stem ends removed, leaves cut into ½-inch lengths and then separated
1 large bunch arugula, washed, dried, and stem ends trimmed
1 large egg
½ cup freshly grated Parmesan cheese

Croutons:

½ cup olive oil
4 1-inch-thick slices day-old French or Italian bread, cut into ½-inch cubes

Caesar Dressing:

1 large garlic clove, minced
6 anchovy fillets, drained and finely chopped
1 tablespoon Dijon mustard
3 tablespoons freshly squeezed lemon juice
1 teaspoon Worcestershire sauce
1 cup virgin olive oil

Prick each sausage in several places with the sharp point of a knife. Bring 1 inch of water to a boil in a saucepan and add the sausages. Simmer them for about 10 minutes, drain and cool.

Put the greens into a large salad bowl and refrigerate them until called for.

Then make the croutons. Heat ¼ cup of

the oil in a large frying pan and cook the bread cubes until crisp and golden brown. Drain them on paper towels and set aside.

Cut the sausages into ¼-inch slices. Heat the remaining ¼ cup olive oil in a clean frying pan and sauté the sausage slices until golden brown on each side. Drain.

To prepare the dressing, whisk the garlic, anchovies, mustard, lemon juice, and Worcestershire sauce together in a small bowl, then drop by drop whisk in the olive oil.

Boil the egg for 1 minute.

Pour the dressing over the greens and toss. Add the toasted croutons and toss. Break the egg over the salad and toss. Add the Parmesan cheese and toss.

Divide the salad evenly among four dinner plates and add a border of the warm sausage slices in equal portions. Serve immediately, and pass the peppermill.

Serves 4

Mixed Greens with Smoked Salmon

Served with a creamy lemon, horseradish, and cracked black pepper dressing and butter-fried croutons, this light but satisfying main course salad serves as a perfect meal on a day that you've already had a substantial lunch or dinner.

1 small bunch arugula, washed, dried, and stem ends trimmed
½ bunch watercress, washed, dried, and stem ends trimmed
1 head red-leaf lettuce, washed, dried, and torn into bite-sized pieces
2 small heads Bibb lettuce, cored, washed, and dried, and torn into bite-sized pieces
12 thin slices smoked salmon

Creamy Lemon, Horseradish, and Cracked Black Pepper Dressing:

2 tablespoons freshly squeezed lemon juice
1 tablespoon white wine vinegar
1 egg yolk, at room temperature
1 teaspoon grated horseradish
⅔ cup virgin olive oil
2 tablespoons heavy cream
Salt and freshly cracked black pepper*

Butter-Fried Croutons:

6 tablespoons clarified butter†
12 ⅓-inch-thick slices French bread

Make the dressing first: Whisk together the lemon juice, vinegar, egg yolk, and horseradish. Drop by drop whisk in the olive oil. Then whisk in the cream, and season to taste with salt and the cracked pepper.

Then make the croutons: Heat the butter in a large frying pan and quickly cook the bread slices over medium heat until golden brown on each side. Drain on paper towels.

Combine the greens in a large bowl, add 4 tablespoons of the dressing, and toss.

Arrange the greens in equal amounts on four dinner plates. Put three salmon slices over each salad. Drizzle the remaining dressing over the salmon equally, and garnish each salad with three fried croutons.

Serves 4

* *To make cracked pepper:* Put a dozen whole black peppercorns on a hard surface, such as a sheet of marble, and crush them gently with the bottom of a small, heavy saucepan.

† *To clarify butter:* Slowly melt the butter over low heat in a saucepan; the white sediment and solids will separate and sink to the bottom of the pan. Slowly pour off the golden liquid butter through a strainer. Leftover clarified butter will keep in a securely covered jar in the refrigerator for a week.

Mixed Greens with Fried Potato Scallops

*F*resh mixed greens with a robust oil and vinegar dressing, flavored with shredded Fontina cheese and topped with buttery crisp fried potato scallops, provides an uncommonly good light meal.

2 cups each bite-sized pieces washed and dried chicory (curly endive) and oakleaf lettuce
2 Belgian endive, stem ends removed, leaves cut into ½-inch lengths and then separated
3 tablespoons sweet butter
1 tablespoon vegetable oil
3 small Idaho potatoes, peeled and very thinly sliced
Salt and freshly ground pepper to taste
Red wine vinegar
Virgin olive oil
3 tablespoons shredded Fontina cheese (use a Mouli grater or a shredder)

Combine the greens in a large bowl.

Heat the butter and oil in a large frying pan, arrange the potatoes in overlapping rows around the pan to form a large circle about 5 inches in diameter, and cook over medium-high heat until golden brown. Carefully turn the potato cake with two large spatulas so that it remains intact, and brown on the other side.

Sprinkle the greens with salt and pepper, drizzle with vinegar and oil to taste, and toss. Add the Fontina cheese and toss again. Divide the greens among four large plates.

Cut the large potato cake into four equal-sized wedges, top each salad with one wedge, and serve immediately.

Serves 4

Watercress and Romaine Salad with Sautéed Chicken Livers and Shallots

*I*f you like chicken livers, you'll love this northern Italian salad served with Grilled Polenta Fingers, a kind of cornmeal cake or bread. Cook the polenta first, prepare the salad while the polenta is cooling, and then grill the polenta fingers.

- *1 bunch watercress, washed, dried, stem ends trimmed*
- *1 medium-sized head romaine lettuce, washed, dried, and torn into bite-sized pieces*

¼ cup butter (4 tablespoons)
Olive oil
24 small whole shallots, peeled
¾ pound chicken livers, coarsely chopped, tendons removed
Salt and freshly ground pepper
Red wine vinegar
1 recipe Grilled Polenta Fingers

Combine the greens in a large bowl.

Heat the butter and 2 tablespoons of the olive oil in a large non-stick frying pan and cook the shallots over medium-low heat for about 10 minutes, stirring often, until tender. Remove them with a slotted spoon and drain.

Add the livers to the pan and cook over medium-high heat for about 5 minutes, stirring often.

Divide the greens evenly among four dinner plates and top each with equal portions of the shallots and livers. Sprinkle with salt and pepper and drizzle a little vinegar and oil over each salad to taste.

Serve immediately with Grilled Polenta Fingers.

Serves 4

Grilled Polenta Fingers

2 cups water
2 cups homemade chicken stock or canned chicken broth
4 cups coarse ground yellow cornmeal
2 teaspoons salt
2 tablespoons butter
Olive oil

Bring the water and stock to a boil in a heavy saucepan. Add the cornmeal slowly, constantly stirring with a wooden spoon until smooth. Reduce the heat to low and cook over low heat, stirring often, for about 45 minutes.

Stir in the salt and butter.

Turn the polenta into a large platter or baking sheet and spread evenly to ½-inch thickness. Let cool for 30 minutes.

When cool, brush olive oil over the polenta and cut it into fingers about 1½ by 3 inches. Grill or cook in batches on a ridged cast-iron skillet over medium-high heat, until the black grill marks appear. This will only take a few moments per side. Serve hot or at room temperature.

Makes about 16 fingers

Arugula and Salami Salad with Parmesan Cheese

Arugula has a unique fresh peppery flavor that I admire so much I often create salads centered around it. This is such a salad, enhanced enormously by the Genoa salami, Parmesan cheese shavings, and balsamic vinaigrette dressing. Serve with crusty Italian bread and sweet butter.

2 large bunches arugula, washed, dried, and stem ends trimmed
2 cups cubed Genoa salami
½ pound piece Parmesan cheese

Balsamic Vinaigrette I:

2 tablespoons balsamic vinegar
2 tablespoons red wine vinegar
½ cup virgin olive oil
1 tablespoon finely chopped fresh basil, or ½ teaspoon dried basil
¼ teaspoon dried oregano
Salt and freshly ground pepper to taste

Make the dressing first by whisking together the vinegars, whisking in the oil drop by drop, stirring in the basil and oregano, and seasoning to taste with salt and pepper.

Put the arugula and salami in a large bowl. Pour half of the dressing over it and toss. Divide the mixture among four dinner plates in equal portions.

Cut the cheese into thin shavings with a very sharp knife or, if you have one, a truffle cutter or shaver. Top each salad with equal amounts of the cheese, spoon the remaining dressing over each, and serve.

Serves 4

PASTA SALADS

*B*ecause pasta is a perfect food for main course salads, as well as my all-time favorite food, it was very difficult for me to limit this chapter to only thirteen pasta salad recipes.

The list of pasta's attributes is long. It is inexpensive, can be made in advance for salads, can easily be cooked in small or large quantities, and can be served warm, at room temperature, or cold. Pasta is a great friend of vegetarians, too. Pasta gives substance to a salad, absorbs flavors well, and comes in as many shapes and sizes, from tiny rice-shaped orzo to plump ridged rigatoni, as anyone could want.

By now we are all familiar with penne, ziti, spaghetti, fusilli, and so on, but I've included a recipe here using radiatore, a less common and very attractive curled radiator-shaped pasta which, when cooked, collects sauce and small bits of foods and absorbs the flavors, and each piece is a perfect bite size.

All dressings, whether oil-and-vinegar, mayonnaise-, or cream-based, enhance pasta, and almost every food and complementary combination can make excellent pasta salads.

Main course pasta salads are great for entertaining, of course, and they are especially efficient for serving crowds, for picnics, tailgates, or box lunches, since pasta is fork food and very portable.

I prefer to use dried imported Italian pasta

for salad-making, since fresh pasta tends to become too soft and limp if not eaten immediately.

Some pasta absorbs more dressing than others, so that sometimes the amount of dressing or sauce that is required differs from the amount given in a recipe. Therefore, it's always a good idea to toss a pasta salad with the dressing, let it rest a few minutes, then retoss it and taste to see if it's moist enough. A small quantity of oil or mayonnaise—whatever the main dressing ingredient is—can be added if necessary.

RECIPES

Shells with Tuna, Toasted Pine Nuts, and Pesto Sauce
Penne with Radicchio, Arugula, New Potatoes, and Fontina
Tuna and Radiatore
Elsa's Curried Rotelle Salad
Cheese Tortellini with Marinated Artichoke Hearts
Bobbe Hart's Antipasto Pasta Salad
Spaghetti and Caviar Igloo Salad
Penne with Broccoli
California Macaroni Salad with Johnnycakes
Farfalle, Fresh Tomato, and Mixed Herb Salad
Ziti and Green Vegetable Primavera Salad
Fusilli and Shrimp with Lemon-Tarragon Dressing
Spaghetti, Fresh Tomato, and Basil Salad

Shells with Tuna, Toasted Pine Nuts, and Pesto Sauce

Shells are used in this dish because there is tuna in the recipe and, of course, shells represent the sea: Poetry in pasta! Actually, the real reason is that the little pockets in each shell collect extra amounts of the fragrant sauce, making every bite moist and more delicious.

Serve with steamed zucchini slices, tossed lightly in a little oil, salt, and freshly ground pepper.

3 quarts water
2 tablespoons butter
½ cup pine nuts
1 tablespoon salt
8 ounces dry medium shells
2 6½-ounce cans solid white-meat tuna packed in oil, drained and flaked
3 tablespoons capers in liquid
2 teaspoons caper liquid from jar

Pesto Sauce:
1 cup fresh basil leaves, packed (dried basil cannot be substituted)
½ cup coarsely chopped fresh parsley
1¼ cups virgin olive oil
1 teaspoon chopped garlic
Salt and freshly ground pepper to taste

Bring the water to a rolling boil in a large pot.

Meanwhile, heat the butter in a frying pan and cook the pine nuts for 1 or 2 minutes over medium-high heat, stirring often, until evenly toasted. Drain on paper towels.

Add the salt to the boiling water, stir, and add the pasta. Stir again and cook the pasta *al dente*, about 6 minutes, or just until tender, stirring often.

While the pasta is cooking, make the pesto sauce: Put the basil, parsley, olive oil, and garlic into the container of a food processor or blender and puree until very smooth. Season to taste with salt and pepper.

Drain the cooked pasta well and transfer it to a large bowl. Add the pesto sauce, tuna, capers and caper liquid, and toasted pine nuts, and toss well.

Serve warm, or cover, refrigerate, and serve cold. Pass the peppermill.

Serves 4

Penne with Radicchio, Arugula, New Potatoes, and Fontina

*I*n this recipe it is necessary for the red radicchio to be simmered slowly for one hour to eliminate any bitterness. While it cooks, most of the other ingredients can be prepared and cooked. Serve with Italian whole wheat bread slices, buttered, broiled, and spread with minced green peppers and onions.

1 cup virgin olive oil
½ teaspoon minced garlic
2 heads radicchio, cored and thinly shredded
8 leaves fresh basil, chopped
¼ teaspoon salt
1 pound small new unpeeled potatoes, cut into ½-inch cubes
3 tablespoons butter
8 whole peeled garlic cloves
Freshly ground pepper
3½ quarts water
1 pound penne (fusilli can be substituted)
1 cup diced seeded fresh ripe but firm Italian plum tomato
½ pound Fontina cheese, diced
1 bunch arugula, washed, dried, and cut into ⅛-inch shreds (watercress can be substituted)
2 tablespoons white wine vinegar or to taste
1 cup heavy cream
½ cup freshly grated Parmesan cheese

Heat ½ cup of the olive oil with the minced garlic in a heavy 2½-quart saucepan. Add the radicchio, basil, and salt to taste. Stir and simmer, partially covered, over very low heat for 1 hour, stirring occasionally.

Meanwhile, heat the remaining ½ cup of oil and the butter in a large frying pan. Add the potatoes and garlic and cook over medium heat until crisp and golden. Drain the potatoes, season them lightly with salt and pepper, and set aside.

When the radicchio has cooked 45 minutes, bring the water to a rolling boil in a large pot, stir in 1 tablespoon of salt, and add the penne. Stir and cook *al dente*, about 8 minutes, stirring often.

While the pasta is cooking, place the tomatoes, cheese, and arugula in a large bowl and gently combine.

Drain the cooked pasta well and add it to the ingredients in the bowl. Sprinkle with the vinegar and toss.

Pour the cream into the pan with the radicchio and bring to a boil.

Immediately pour the mixture over the pasta; add the Parmesan cheese and combine well.

Season to taste with salt and pepper and serve immediately.

Serves 6

Tuna and Radiatore

Radiatore's unusual curly shape makes a lovely presentation, but, best of all, the many little ridges and curls of each bite-sized pasta morsel hold and absorb hearty sauces beautifully. Radiatore can be found in both specialty food shops and supermarkets. If unavailable, you can replace it with ziti or penne.

This marvelous salad is a combination of flavors and textures: pasta, tuna, crisp carrots and celery, and creamy sauce accented with cucumber slices. A perfect accompaniment is thick slices of tomato, sprinkled with fresh chopped basil and olive oil, and Italian bread and sweet butter.

3 quarts water
1 tablespoon salt
8 ounces dry radiatore
2 tablespoons olive oil
1 tablespoon lemon juice
1 cup mayonnaise or Classic Mayonnaise (page 128)
¼ cup minced red onion
1 6½-ounce can solid white-meat tuna packed in oil, flaked but not drained
1 cup grated fresh peeled carrot
½ cup diced celery
Salt and freshly ground pepper
2 small unpeeled cucumbers, thinly sliced

Bring the water to a rolling boil. Add the salt, stir, and add the pasta. Cook the pasta *al dente*, stirring often, for about 10 minutes.

Meanwhile, in a large bowl combine the olive oil, lemon juice, and mayonnaise with a wire whisk. Stir in the tuna and oil from the can, add carrots and celery, and season to taste with salt and pepper.

Drain the cooked pasta, add to the tuna mixture, and toss well.

The salad can be served warm, at room temperature, or chilled. Spoon equal amounts onto four dinner plates and surround each salad with equal amounts of the sliced cucumber.

For a curried variation, add 1 tablespoon of freshly grated orange rind, 1 tablespoon of curry powder, and ¼ teaspoon of turmeric to the mayonnaise mixture in recipe.

Serves 4

Elsa's Curried Rotelle Salad

*T*his salad, which features rotelle, a wheel-shaped pasta, is a great summer meal, served with Italian bread.

3 quarts water
8 ounces dry rotelle
1 tablespoon salt
1 tablespoon fresh grated orange peel
⅔ cup raisins
1¼ cups fresh peas or 1 10-ounce package
    frozen green peas, cooked and drained
½ cup chopped bread and butter pickles
3 scallions, thinly sliced
½ cup chopped sun-dried tomato
1 large Delicious apple, cored and cut into
    1-inch cubes
4 tablespoons butter
Salt and freshly ground pepper to taste

Curried Mayonnaise I:

¾ cup mayonnaise or Classic Mayonnaise
    (page 128)
¼ cup olive oil
Juice of 1 lemon
1 tablespoon curry powder
½ teaspoon turmeric
Salt and freshly ground pepper to taste

Bring the water to a rolling boil in a large pot. Add the salt, stir, and add the pasta. Stir the pasta, and cook it *al dente*, or just until tender, about 6 minutes, stirring it often.

Meanwhile, make the dressing: Combine the mayonnaise, olive oil, lemon juice, curry powder, and turmeric in a large bowl with a wire whisk. Season with salt and pepper.

Add the remaining ingredients, except for the butter, and combine.

Drain the pasta and transfer it to a large bowl. Add the butter and toss well.

Turn the combined ingredients over the pasta and toss. Season to taste with salt and pepper.

The salad can be served warm, or cool it, covered, in the refrigerator for several hours, then before serving, bring it to room temperature and toss it again.

Serves 4

Cheese Tortellini with Marinated Artichoke Hearts

*A*rtichoke hearts preserved in jars in a marinade of oil, vinegar, herbs, and spices retain their delicate flavor quite well, and add a nice zing to salads. Here the marinated artichokes provide a pleasant contrast to cheese-filled tortellini, making an unusually good main course salad that is very easy. If desired, serve with sliced tomatoes sprinkled lightly with olive oil, minced anchovies, garlic, and freshly ground pepper.

3 quarts water
1 tablespoon salt
3 6-ounce jars marinated artichoke hearts, drained (reserve marinade for dressing)
¼ cup diced pimiento
8 ounces cheese-filled tortellini
2 tablespoons chopped fresh basil
2 tablespoons chopped fresh parsley
Salt and freshly ground pepper to taste

Parmesan Vinaigrette Dressing:

1 tablespoon white wine vinegar
¼ cup extra-virgin olive oil
Artichoke marinade from jars
2 tablespoons freshly grated Parmesan cheese
Salt and freshly ground pepper to taste

Bring the water to a rolling boil in a large pot.

Meanwhile, put the artichoke hearts and pimientos into a large bowl.

In a small bowl make the dressing: Whisk together the vinegar and the oil, drop by drop. Drop by drop whisk in the artichoke marinade, and finally, whisk in the cheese. Season to taste with salt and pepper.

Add the salt to the boiling water in the pot, stir, add the pasta, and stir again. Cook the tortellini *al dente*, about 5 minutes, or just until tender, stirring often.

Drain the cooked pasta and add it to the bowl with the artichoke hearts and pimientos. Pour the dressing over the top and combine well. Add the basil and parsley, and season to taste with salt and pepper.

Serve the salad warm or at room temperature, or cover and refrigerate until well chilled. Toss again, and serve chilled.

Serves 4

Bobbe Hart's Antipasto Pasta Salad

My St. Thomas neighbor and friend, Bobbe Hart, has enjoyed cooking and creating recipes for years, especially pasta, and she has generously shared a number of her inventions with me. These exchanges often take place over the backyard fence as we garden and water our plants, flowers, and fruit trees and chat. It's a lovely ritual that is becoming extinct. This tasty recipe can easily be cut in half to serve four. Or, as Bobbe says, just cut the salad ingredients in half and make the whole dressing recipe. The extra dressing can be stored in the refrigerator for several days in a tightly covered jar and used as a marinade or baste for broiled chicken or fish. Serve the salad with crusty Italian bread and sweet butter.

3½ quarts water
1 pound dry linguine
1 tablespoon salt
¼ cup freshly grated Parmesan cheese or as needed
¼ cup chopped fresh parsley
3 tablespoons chopped fresh basil
½ cup minced red onion
Freshly ground pepper to taste
1 green bell pepper, cored, seeded, and cut into julienne strips
1 yellow bell pepper, cored, seeded, and cut into julienne strips
1 pint cherry tomatoes, halved
½ pound Genoa salami or mortadella, cut into 1½-inch cubes
½ pound boiled ham, cut into ½-inch cubes
½ pound Swiss cheese, cut into ½-inch cubes
16 pitted giant black olives, quartered

1 large head romaine lettuce, washed, dried, and torn into bite-sized pieces

Zesty Salad Dressing:

(Makes about 3 cups)
1½ cups vegetable oil
½ cup virgin olive oil
⅔ cup white wine vinegar
2 garlic cloves, minced
2 teaspoons dried oregano
2 teaspoons dried basil
½ teaspoon dried thyme
½ teaspoon paprika
¼ cup freshly grated Parmesan cheese
1 tablespoon sugar
2 teaspoons salt (optional)
Freshly ground pepper to taste

Bring the water to a rolling boil, stir in the salt, and add the pasta. Stir again, and cook al dente, about 6 minutes, or just until tender, stirring often.

While the pasta cooks, make the dressing: Shake all of the ingredients together in a quart jar with a tight-fitting lid.

Drain the pasta and rinse it briefly in cold tap water. Transfer the pasta to a large bowl, moisten it with ½ cup of the dressing, and toss. Add the Parmesan cheese, parsley, basil, red onion, and pepper to taste. Toss, cover, and let stand at room temperature until ready to serve.

Just prior to serving, add all the remaining ingredients except the lettuce, and combine. Shake the dressing and add it, half a cup at a time, as needed. Toss and taste for seasoning.

Line eight plates with the romaine pieces and spoon equal amounts of the salad on top.

Serves 8

Spaghetti and Caviar Igloo Salad

A little caviar goes a long way when combined with spaghetti in this delectable fantasy salad. Red lumpfish caviar is used, which is inexpensive when compared to its very distant royal relative, Beluga. (Beluga should never be mixed with anything except perhaps a few drops of lemon juice and savored on toast.)

Here the spaghetti is tossed in a mixture of lumpfish caviar, crème fraîche (made a day in advance), lemon juice, scallions, and pepper, chilled in cups, then inverted onto plates, making little igloos, and surrounded with greens that have been lightly coated with a piquant dressing. Serve with bread-sticks or Italian bread and butter and a dry white wine or champagne.

3 quarts water
1 tablespoon salt
8 ounces dry spaghetti
1 cup crème fraîche*
2 scallions, thinly sliced
1 tablespoon freshly squeezed lemon juice, or to taste
2 ounces red lumpfish caviar
Freshly ground pepper
Vegetable oil
1 bunch watercress, washed, dried, and stemmed
4 Belgian endive, stem ends removed, leaves cut into ½-inch lengths and then separated
2 teaspoons chopped fresh parsley

Dressing:

2 tablespoons white wine vinegar
2 teaspoons Dijon mustard
½ cup virgin olive oil
2 tablespoons walnut oil
Salt and freshly ground pepper to taste

Bring the water to a rolling boil in a large pot. Add the salt, stir, and add the pasta. Stir and cook the pasta *al dente*, or just until tender, about 6 minutes, stirring often.

Meanwhile, combine the crème fraîche, scallions, lemon juice, caviar, and pepper in a large bowl.

Drain the spaghetti, add to the bowl, and toss well.

Generously oil four over-sized curved coffee cups. Twirl several forkfuls of the spaghetti into each cup in equal amounts (all pasta should be used). Spoon the remaining sauce in the bottom of the bowl over the spaghetti in equal portions. Cover and chill the cups of spaghetti for several hours.

To make the dressing, whisk together the vinegar and mustard, drop by drop whisk in the oils, and season to taste with salt and pepper.

Combine the watercress and endive in a bowl, pour the dressing over the greens, and toss.

Invert each cup of spaghetti onto an individual dinner plate and shake once to release. If necessary, run a knife along the sides of the spaghetti and the cup to release any sticking. Spoon equal portions of the salad greens around the igloos and sprinkle with the parsley. Serve immediately.

Serves 4

* *To make crème fraîche:* Whisk together 1 cup of heavy cream and 1 cup of sour cream in a Mason-type jar with a tight-fitting lid. Cover the jar and let the mixture stand at room temperature for about 8 hours or until thickened. Refrigerate until needed. Crème fraîche will keep stored in the refrigerator for 4 days. Yields 2 cups.

Penne with Broccoli

*T*his garlic-laced salad can be enjoyed by vegetarians and nonvegetarians alike. Serve with warmed slices of Italian bread topped with Bel Paese or provolone cheese. The bread can be spread lightly with virgin olive oil or sweet butter first and toasted.

3½ quarts water
¾ cup olive oil
1½ tablespoons minced garlic
1 tablespoon salt
1 pound dry penne
1 stick melted sweet butter
6 cups chopped fresh broccoli, or 3 10-ounce
     packages frozen chopped broccoli
Salt and freshly ground pepper to taste

Bring 3½ quarts of water to a rolling boil in a large pot.

Meanwhile, heat the olive oil slowly with the garlic in a large frying pan for 5 minutes, stirring occasionally.

Add the salt to the boiling water in the pot, stir, and add the pasta. Stir and cook *al dente*, or just until tender, about 8 minutes, stirring occasionally.

If using fresh broccoli, bring 1 quart of lightly salted water to a boil, add the broccoli, and cook until just tender, about 5 minutes. (If using frozen broccoli, cook according to package instructions.) Drain the cooked broccoli well.

Add the broccoli to the frying pan with the oil, garlic, and melted butter, and turn gently to coat evenly.

Drain the pasta and transfer it to a large bowl. Top it with the broccoli mixture and season to taste with salt and pepper. Serve warm or at room temperature.

Serves 8

California Macaroni Salad with Johnnycakes

Classic macaroni salad has three requirements: It must be creamy, the vegetables must be crisp, and it has to be served cold. This California version is updated a bit with fennel, baby corn, artichoke hearts, and sugar snap peas, but the wonderful original qualities remain intact.

Johnnycakes make a perfect accompaniment.

1 red bell pepper, cored, seeded, and diced
1 cup diced celery

½ cup diced fennel
½ cup diced red onion
½ cup diced and seeded tomato
12 jarred baby corns, drained
8 marinated jarred artichoke hearts, chopped
12 sugar snap peas, stemmed and stringed, blanched and cut into julienne strips lengthwise (blanched snow peas can be substituted)
3 quarts water
1 tablespoon salt
2 cups dry macaroni
Salt and freshly ground pepper to taste
1 recipe Johnnycakes (page 78)
1¼ cups mayonnaise or Classic Mayonnaise (page 128)
3 tablespoons vinegar
1 tablespoon Dijon mustard
1 tablespoon sugar
¼ cup heavy cream
Salt and freshly ground pepper to taste

Combine vegetables in a large bowl.

Bring the water to a rolling boil in a large pot, add the salt, stir, add the macaroni, stir, and cook just until tender, about 8 minutes.

Meanwhile, combine the remaining ingredients in a bowl.

Drain the macaroni, add it to the vegetables, turn the dressing over the top, and combine all the ingredients well. Season to taste with salt and pepper.

Cool the salad, cover and refrigerate for several hours. Toss again and serve cold with hot or warm johnnycakes. (The salad can be made a day ahead.)
Serves 4

Johnnycakes

Johnnycakes are small West Indian fried bread *cakes*. They are a delicious and welcome addition to any meal, best eaten while still hot or warm. They are also wonderful breakfast treats, split open and slathered with butter and jam or preserves.

2 cups all-purpose flour
2 teaspoons baking powder
½ teaspoon salt
1 tablespoon sugar
½ cup vegetable shortening
¼ cup evaporated milk
¼ cup water
Peanut or vegetable oil for frying

Sift the dry ingredients together in a large bowl. Cut in the shortening with a pastry cutter until a coarse crumb texture is reached. Add the milk and water and mix into a dough. Knead the dough for 5 minutes by hand and shape into a ball. Cover and let rest to rise for 30 minutes.

Shape the dough into balls about the size of small limes. Flatten to about ½ inch thick with the palms of your hands.

Fry the johnnycakes, a few at a time, in 2 inches of hot oil in a deep pot or frying-pan, until golden brown on both sides.

Drain on paper towels and serve while still hot or warm.
Makes 12

Farfalle, Fresh Tomato, and Mixed Herb Salad

This unusually light summer salad can also be turned into a side dish salad for variety for a dinner party for six. Heat up the outdoor barbecue and cook a mixed grill entrée of lamb chops, sausages, and chicken.

Parmesan Crostini is a very good crunchy side dish for this aromatic salad. To make them, cut 16 ¼-inch-thick slices of Italian or French bread and spread each lightly with butter on one side. Sprinkle them lightly with freshly grated Parmesan cheese and pass under the broiler on a baking sheet until lightly toasted.

3 quarts water
1 tablespoon salt
10 firm ripe Italian plum tomatoes
12 ounces dry farfalle (bowtie-shaped pasta),
    or medium shells
1 cup chopped washed, dried, and stemmed
    arugula
3 tablespoons chopped fresh basil
3 tablespoons chopped fresh parsley
2 tablespoons chopped fresh dill, or 1 teaspoon
    dried dill
1 teaspoon chopped fresh thyme, or ½ teaspoon
    dried thyme
Salt and freshly ground pepper

Italian Dressing:

3 tablespoons white wine vinegar or to taste
1 garlic clove, peeled and minced
¾ cup olive oil
Salt and freshly ground pepper to taste

Bring the water to a rolling boil in a large pot.

Add the salt to the boiling water, stir, and add the pasta. Cook the pasta al dente, about 6 minutes, or just until tender, stirring often.

Meanwhile, trim off the stem ends from the tomatoes, cut the tomatoes in half crosswise, and squeeze out the seeds and pulp. Dice the tomatoes and put them into a large bowl.

While the pasta cooks, add the arugula and herbs to the bowl with the tomatoes and combine.

Make the dressing: Whisk together the vinegar and garlic, drop by drop whisk in the oil, then season to taste with salt and pepper.

Drain the cooked pasta well, put into the bowl with the tomatoes, arugula, and herbs, and combine. Pour the dressing over the pasta. Season to taste with salt and pepper.

This salad can be served hot, warm, or cold. If serving it warm or cold, be sure to toss it again before serving.

Serves 4

Ziti and Green Vegetable Primavera Salad

*P*asta Primavera has been very popular for almost a decade in this country, with good reason. The combination of pasta and fragrant vegetables bathed in a creamy aromatic sauce or dressing is a marriage made in heaven. Here's my latest favorite version. Serve it with toasted Italian bread slices lightly spread with finely chopped, seeded and drained tomatoes and red onion combined with a little olive oil.

1½ cups cooked chopped broccoli
1 cup cooked green beans, cut into 1-inch lengths
1¼ cups fresh-cooked green peas, well-drained, or 1 10-ounce package frozen green peas, cooked and drained
6 cooked asparagus spears, cut into 1-inch lengths
24 snow pea pods, stemmed, strings removed, blanched, and drained
3 tablespoons chopped fresh parsley
3 tablespoons chopped fresh basil
¼ cup thinly sliced scallions
3 quarts water
1 tablespoon salt
8 ounces dry ziti (penne can be substituted)
Salt and freshly ground pepper to taste
½ cup olive oil
1 teaspoon minced garlic
¼ teaspoon hot pepper flakes (optional)
1 cup heavy cream or as needed
½ cup freshly grated Parmesan cheese

Put all the ingredients through the scallions into a large bowl and gently combine.

Bring the water to a rolling boil. Add the salt, stir, add the pasta, and stir. Cook the pasta *al dente*, about 8 minutes, or just until tender, stirring frequently.

Meanwhile, make the sauce: Heat ¼ cup of the oil in a small frying pan and add the garlic. Cook over medium heat for 2 minutes, stir in the pepper flakes, if desired, and set aside.

In a saucepan bring the cream to a boil. Stir in the cheese and cook for 1 minute, whisking often. Remove from the heat, stir in the garlic–pepper flakes mixture and Parmesan cheese, and the remaining oil, and season to taste with salt and pepper.

Drain the spaghetti lightly and turn into a large bowl. Add half of the cream sauce and half of the vegetables, and toss lightly. Add the remaining vegetables and sauce, and toss. Season to taste with salt, pepper, and extra Parmesan cheese, if necessary. If the salad is not moist enough, add a little more cream.

Serve the salad warm or at room temperature, or cover and refrigerate until well chilled. If chilled, bring the salad back to room temperature before serving it and toss again.

Serves 4

Fusilli and Shrimp with Lemon-Tarragon Dressing

*T*arragon is an herb that is generally not associated with pasta dishes, but it makes a perfect union in this lemon-scented shrimp dish. Serve with grilled slices of eggplant, zucchini, and bell peppers.

1 pound raw medium shrimp, shelled and
   deveined
4 tablespoons butter
1 tablespoon freshly squeezed lemon juice
3 quarts water
1 tablespoon salt
8 ounces dry fusilli
Salt and freshly ground pepper to taste

Lemon-Tarragon Dressing:

2 tablespoons tarragon vinegar
2 tablespoons freshly squeezed lemon juice
1 tablespoon Dijon mustard
½ cup olive oil
½ cup vegetable oil
Salt and freshly ground pepper to taste
1 tablespoon chopped fresh tarragon, or
   1 teaspoon dried tarragon
1 shallot, minced

Cut each shrimp in half lengthwise. (When shrimp are cut in this manner, they curl up when cooked, producing a very attractive corkscrew shape.)

Heat the butter and lemon juice together in a large frying pan and cook the shrimp over medium-low heat for about 6 minutes, turning often. Set aside.

Bring the water to a rolling boil. Add the salt, stir, add the pasta, and stir. Cook the pasta *al dente*, about 6 minutes, or just until tender, stirring often.

Meanwhile, make the dressing: Whisk together the vinegar, lemon juice, and mustard; drop by drop whisk in the oils, then season to taste with salt and pepper. Stir in the tarragon and shallot.

Drain the pasta and put it into a large bowl. Add the shrimp and dressing, and combine thoroughly. Season to taste with salt and pepper. Cover and refrigerate for several hours.

Remove the salad from the refrigerator 30 minutes before serving to come back to room temperature. Toss before serving.

Serves 4

Spaghetti, Fresh Tomato, and Basil Salad

*T*his pasta salad utilizes summer's beautiful, bountiful fresh tomatoes and fragrant basil, perhaps from your own garden. For a cooling dinner, begin with melon and prosciutto, and offer a fresh berry tart for dessert.

4 firm ripe Italian or summer tomatoes
½ cup chopped fresh basil
¼ cup chopped fresh parsley
1 teaspoon minced garlic
½ cup extra-virgin olive oil
3 tablespoons white wine vinegar
2 tablespoons freshly squeezed lemon juice
Salt and freshly ground pepper to taste
3 quarts water
1 tablespoon salt
8 ounces dry spaghetti

Cut the tomatoes in half crosswise and squeeze out the seeds. Dice the tomatoes, discarding the stem ends.

Put the diced tomatoes into a bowl and add all the ingredients through the lemon juice. Season well with salt and pepper to taste.

Bring the water to a rolling boil in a large pot, add the salt, and stir. Add the pasta, stir, and cook *al dente*, or just until tender, about 6 minutes, stirring frequently.

Drain the cooked pasta well and pass it under cold tap water for about 10 seconds.

Put the spaghetti in a bowl, add the tomato mixture, and toss well. Taste for seasoning.

Serve at room temperature, or cover and chill for one hour. Toss again before serving.

Serves 4

POTATO AND RICE SALADS

*P*otatoes and rice can be turned into many new main course salads because, like pasta, they are so versatile: They each retain their own individual characteristics of flavor and texture while absorbing other flavors and accepting many other foods.

Another virtue of potatoes and rice is that compositions based on either one can be molded into individual or large timbals, terrines, or other shaped molds, bound by creamy or vinegar-and-oil-based dressings, for an attractive presentation.

To spark your imagination, here are examples of two interesting molded salads I have made, one of potatoes and one of rice. I once lined one-cup ramekins with poached leek leaves and filled the centers with a cubed roast beef and potato salad with a sweetened mayonnaise and caraway seed dressing. The ends of the leek leaves were folded up over the top of each ramekin and the salads were then well chilled. Inverted onto individual plates, the salads were garnished with sautéed, thinly sliced celery and sprinkled with a mixture of chopped fresh herbs.

Another time I tossed cooked rice, shrimp, and diced cooked young zucchini, carrots, and peppers, in basil vinaigrette, chilled the mixture in a terrine, and turned it out onto a platter, surrounded by watercress and slivered endive. It worked beautifully.

Remember to take care not to overcook

potatoes or they will crumble and instantly ruin a salad. Also, potatoes must always be drained well. Cooked rice should separate easily, but at the same time, it should not be too dry.

The potato and rice recipes in this chapter are all favorites of mine, old and new, that make exceptionally good main courses for every season of the year.

RECIPES

New Potato and Red Salmon Caviar Salad with Endive
Provençale Potato and Kielbasa Salad
German Potato and Chicken Salad with Bacon
Nasi Goreng
Paella Salad
Curried Wild Pecan Rice with Chicken and Pecans
Wild Rice, Lobster, and Asparagus Salad
Rice and Vegetable Salad with Shrimp
Risi e Bisi Salad on Canadian Bacon and Fried Croutons
Rice and Black Bean Salad with Sautéed Bananas

New Potato and Red Salmon Caviar Salad with Endive

*L*ast year, in honor of the Long Island potato harvest, I decided that a special potato salad for lunch on Labor Day was in order. I found just-dug new potatoes at Babinskys' farmstand, a wonderful local market. Here is the delicious salad we ate, accompanied by cooked broccoli spears, French bread and sweet butter, champagne, and for dessert, fresh sliced peaches showered with a little sugar.

*2 pounds small new potatoes, washed and
    unpeeled*
1 cup sour cream
3 tablespoons chopped fresh dill
1 tablespoon freshly squeezed lemon juice
6 scallions, thinly sliced
*1 2-ounce jar red salmon caviar (red lumpfish
    can be substituted)*
Salt and freshly ground pepper to taste
*4 large Belgian endive, stem ends removed,
    leaves separated*

Cook the new potatoes covered with boiling water for about 12 minutes or just until tender.

Meanwhile, combine the sour cream, dill, lemon juice, scallions, and caviar in a large bowl.

Drain the potatoes and with the aid of a small sharp knife, scrape off the peels. Cut the potatoes into ¼-inch-thick slices and add them to the caviar mixture immediately. Combine well, and season to taste with salt and pepper. (Go easy on the salt because of the salt in the caviar.)

Cover and chill the salad for 2 hours.

Just before serving, arrange the endive leaves in equal amounts on each of four plates in a sunburst pattern, with the pointed ends of the endive leaves facing out. Gently toss the salad again and spoon equal amounts of the mixture over the center of the endive leaves on each plate.

Serves 4

Provençale Potato and Kielbasa Salad

Normally, potato salads are mixed; this one is composed in alternating layers of warm potatoes and sausage slices. A Provençale scented dressing flavors the salad. It's served warm. Since this salad travels well, it's great for outdoor gatherings such as backyard barbecues and picnics or when supplying a dish for dinner at a friend's home. It has become a ritual for us in the summertime, when our weekend dining usually means at least eight people: Just double the recipe.

Serve with pumpernickel sandwiches spread with mustard and filled with watercress and thinly sliced tomatoes.

2 pounds new potatoes, about the same size in diameter as the sausage
Salt
2 pounds kielbasa
2 tablespoons vegetable oil
1 chilled 15-ounce jar red and yellow peppers marinated in brine, drained, patted dry, and cut into ¼-inch-thick strips

Provençale Dressing:

3 tablespoons white wine vinegar
1 tablespoon Dijon mustard
1 teaspoon Worcestershire sauce
1 garlic clove, minced
2 shallots, minced
½ teaspoon dried thyme
½ teaspoon dried marjoram
1 teaspoon dried basil
1 tablespoon chopped fresh parsley
½ teaspoon celery salt
¾ cup olive oil
Salt and freshly ground pepper to taste

Cook the potatoes covered with slowly boiling, lightly salted water for about 12 minutes or until just tender. Drain and cool.

Meanwhile, prepare the dressing: Whisk together the vinegar, mustard, Worcestershire sauce, garlic, shallots, herbs and celery salt in a medium bowl, drop by drop whisk in the olive oil, then season to taste with salt and pepper.

Cut the warm potatoes into ¼-inch-thick slices and remove and discard the peels.

Cut the sausage into ¼-inch-thick slices. Heat the oil in a frying pan, and cook sausage slices in batches until browned. Drain on paper towels.

In a large au gratin dish or shallow baking dish, make rows of alternating slices of the potatoes and sausages.

Whisk the dressing again and spoon it over the salad. Serve warm. Just before serving, make a border of pepper strips around the dish.

Serves 4

German Potato and Chicken Salad with Bacon

*T*his German-style potato and chicken salad, accented with caraway seeds, bacon, and green pepper, is an outstanding main course salad. It's also a great way to use up leftover chicken or turkey. Serve with steamed green beans and iced beer, if desired.

  1½ pounds warm boiled potatoes, peeled and
    cubed
  1½ cups chopped cooked light and dark meat
    chicken
  8 crisp cooked bacon strips, crumbled
  ⅓ cup minced cored and seeded green bell
    pepper
  1 teaspoon caraway seed
  3 tablespoons chopped fresh parsley

Warm Vinaigrette Dressing:

  ⅓ cup white wine vinegar
  ¼ cup minced shallot
  ¾ cup vegetable oil
  1 tablespoon Dijon mustard
  Salt and freshly ground pepper to taste

Put the potatoes, chicken, bacon, and green pepper into a large bowl and toss.

Then make the dressing: Bring the vinegar and shallots to a boil in a saucepan. Whisk in the oil and bring to a boil again. Immediately remove from the heat, whisk in the mustard, and season to taste with salt and pepper.

Pour the dressing over the salad ingredients, add the caraway seeds and parsley, and gently combine. Taste for seasoning.

The salad should be served warm.

Serves 4

Nasi Goreng

*N*asi Goreng is a sumptuous Indonesian fried rice salad composed of the contrasting flavors and textures of shrimp and pork strips, fried shallot slivers, and stir-fried vegetables, topped with a crisp fried egg. This recipe is an adaptation of the superb Nasi Goreng that we sampled at the beautiful beachside resort hotel the Bali Oberoi, in Bali, a few years ago.

Cold beer goes very well with Nasi Goreng.

2½ cups cold cooked long-grain rice (1 cup uncooked rice)
¼ cup soy sauce
1 tablespoon Oriental sesame oil
2 teaspoons sugar
½ cup canned chicken broth
Peanut oil
1 cup thinly sliced shallot
12 snow pea pods, stems and strings removed, cut into bite-sized pieces on the diagonal
1 cup thinly shredded bok choy
½ cup thinly sliced cored and seeded red bell pepper
½ cup thinly sliced celery
4 scallions, cut into ½-inch lengths
1 cup thinly sliced medium-sized raw shrimp (cut lengthwise)
¾ cup thinly shredded raw pork
1 cup bean sprouts
¼ teaspoon hot pepper flakes
2 tablespoons butter
4 large eggs

Fluff up the cold rice with a fork and place next to the stove in a large bowl.

Combine the soy sauce, sesame oil, sugar, and chicken broth in a small bowl and set aside.

Heat 1 inch of the oil to 370° in a deep medium-sized saucepan and cook the shallots for a few minutes until golden brown. Drain and set aside.

Heat 3 tablespoons of the oil in a large wok or frying pan with curved sides until quite hot but not smoking. Add the snow peas, bok choy, pepper, and celery and stir-fry for 1 minute. Add the scallions and stir-fry for 30 seconds.

With a large slotted spoon transfer the fried vegetables to the bowl with the rice.

Add 1 tablespoon of the oil to the wok or frying pan and stir-fry the shrimp and pork for 1 minute. Add the bean sprouts and hot pepper flakes and stir-fry for 30 seconds.

Now, very quickly, add the rice and stir-fried vegetables, the shallots, and the soy sauce combination to the wok, toss, and stir-fry for 1 minute over high heat.

Heat the butter in a large frying pan and fry the eggs on one side only until they are golden brown around the edges but the yolks are still runny.

Divide the salad among four large dinner plates, top each salad with a fried egg, and serve hot.

Serves 4

Paella Salad

Quite honestly, this hearty recipe is simply cold paella. I decided to include it in this collection because we have a salad-loving friend to whom I once served leftover paella and he liked it so much that he always requests "that fantastic paella salad."

The salad improves the second day, so I suggest preparing it a day in advance. Serve it with crusty Italian or French bread and sweet butter and a dry red Spanish wine.

3 sweet Italian sausages
2 large boneless chicken breasts with skin, cut into small pieces
Salt and freshly ground pepper
½ cup olive oil
3 1-inch-thick lean loin pork chops, boned and cut into bite-sized pieces
¾ cup chopped yellow onion
1 large garlic clove, minced
1 green bell pepper, cored, seeded, and diced
1 cup peeled, seeded, and diced tomato
¼ teaspoon ground saffron
1 teaspoon paprika
⅛ teaspoon hot pepper flakes
Salt and freshly ground pepper to taste
3½ cups homemade chicken stock or canned chicken broth
1½ cups raw long-grain rice

¾ pound medium-sized raw shrimp, shelled, deveined, and chopped
1 10-ounce package frozen green peas, thawed
½ cup pimiento strips

Prick the sausages in several places with the point of a sharp knife and simmer them in 1 inch of water in a saucepan for 10 minutes.

Meanwhile, pat the chicken pieces dry and season with salt and pepper. Heat ¼ cup of the oil in a large frying pan and cook the chicken over medium-high heat for about 10 minutes, turning after 5 minutes. Transfer the chicken to a bowl.

Drain and cool the sausages.

Add the remaining ¼ cup of olive oil to the frying pan and stir-fry the pork cubes, onion, garlic, and pepper for 5 minutes over medium heat.

Add the tomatoes, saffron, paprika, and red pepper flakes and season with salt and pepper to taste. Simmer for 10 minutes.

Preheat the oven to 400°.

Cut the sausages into ¼-inch-thick slices.

Bring the chicken stock to a boil in a saucepan.

In a shallow 4-quart paella pan, casserole, or baking dish, spread the pork mixture and add the rice, sausage, chicken, and green peas. Pour the boiling stock over the ingredients and gently stir.

Press the shrimp down into the mixture and bake for about 30 minutes, or until the rice is tender. Remove from the oven and cool for 30 minutes.

Gently fold in the pimientos and let rest for 15 minutes. Fluff the mixture with two forks, cover, and refrigerate for at least 4 hours; overnight is better. Serve cold or bring to room temperature.

Serves 6

Curried Wild Pecan Rice with Chicken and Pecans

Wild pecan rice contains neither wild rice nor pecans; it is a specially developed long-grain rice from Louisiana that has an unusual nutty aroma and flavor that is reminiscent of pecans.

The rice is especially good flavored with curry, and, naturally, pecans. Serve with lightly buttered, toasted firm white bread, crusts trimmed off, cut into triangles, and sliced cooked fresh beets.

2 cups water
1 teaspoon salt
1 tablespoon butter
1 7-ounce package Konriko brand raw wild pecan rice (available in specialty food stores or supermarkets)
1 8-ounce jar marinated artichoke hearts, chopped and drained
1½ cups cubed cooked chicken
¾ cup thinly sliced celery
¾ cup whole pecan halves
1 cup mayonnaise or Classic Mayonnaise (page 128)
¼ cup heavy cream
1½ teaspoons curry powder
1 tablespoon freshly squeezed lemon juice
Salt and freshly ground pepper to taste

Bring the water to a boil in a 2½ quart saucepan. Stir in the salt and butter and add the rice. Stir, cover, and simmer for about 20 minutes or until tender.

Cool the rice.

Put the rice, artichoke hearts, chicken, celery, and pecans into a large bowl and gently combine.

Mix together the mayonnaise, cream, curry powder, lemon juice, salt and pepper, turn over the salad, and combine well. Serve immediately.

Serves 4

Wild Rice, Lobster, and Asparagus Salad

*T*he four ingredients starring in this supreme salad—wild rice, lobster, asparagus, and walnut oil—are among the world's favorite foods; aristocrats all. The result here is, perhaps, the ultimate main course salad.

For an elegant celebration dinner, serve with warmed French bread, sweet butter, and dry white wine or champagne.

> 3 cups homemade chicken stock or canned chicken broth
> 1 cup raw wild rice
> 3 cups water
> Salt
> 16 asparagus stalks, stems peeled, cut into 1-inch lengths on the diagonal
> 2 cups cooked lobster (page 181), cut into bite-sized pieces
> 1 tablespoon chopped fresh parsley

Walnut Oil and Lemon Dressing:

> 3 tablespoons freshly squeezed lemon juice
> 1 tablespoon balsamic vinegar
> 1 tablespoon minced shallot
> ¼ cup walnut oil
> ¼ cup vegetable oil
> Salt and freshly ground pepper to taste

Bring the chicken stock to a boil in a saucepan. Add the wild rice and bring back to the boil. Reduce the heat to a simmer and cook for 45 minutes or until the rice is tender. Drain the rice in a colander.

Lightly salt the water and bring to a boil. Add the asparagus and cook at a low boil for exactly 5 minutes. Drain and refresh under cold running water. Drain well.

To make the dressing, whisk the lemon juice, vinegar, and shallots together in a bowl. Drop by drop whisk in the oils, then season to taste with salt and pepper.

Combine the rice, asparagus, lobster, and parsley in a large bowl. Pour the dressing over the salad and lightly toss. Taste for seasoning. Serve immediately, or cover and refrigerate for several hours. Toss and serve cold.

Serves 4

Rice and Vegetable Salad with Shrimp

*T*his beautiful, fragrant salad can be prepared in advance, which makes it great for entertaining. (The shrimp can be omitted, if desired.) Complete the meal with toasted French bread, sweet butter, and fresh seasonal fruit, with cheese if you like.

1 cup diced cooked peeled carrot
1 cup cooked fresh or frozen green peas
½ cup diced cored and seeded red or yellow bell pepper
½ cup diced seeded firm ripe tomato
½ cup diced peeled and seeded cucumber
1 tablespoon freshly chopped chives, or 1 teaspoon freeze-dried chives
1 pound cooked shelled and deveined medium shrimp (page 184), drained and coarsely chopped
4 cups cooked rice, at room temperature or chilled (approximately 1¾ cups uncooked rice)
12 endive leaves, cut into thin strips lengthwise

Basil Vinaigrette:

3 tablespoons white wine vinegar
2 teaspoons minced shallots
1 cup virgin olive oil or as needed, plus extra for oiling the mold
⅓ cup finely chopped fresh basil
Salt and freshly ground pepper to taste

Combine all the salad ingredients except the endive in a large bowl.

To make the dressing, whisk together the vinegar and shallots, drop by drop whisk in the oil, add the basil, and combine well.

Season to taste with salt and pepper.

Sprinkle the dressing over the salad and mix thoroughly. The salad should be moist, but not wet. Add a little extra oil if needed. Taste for seasoning if extra oil is added.

Turn the salad into a lightly oiled 2-quart terrine or shallow bowl or dish. Press the ingredients gently but firmly down and smooth the top evenly. Cover and refrigerate the salad for at least 1 hour.

To turn out, invert the salad onto a platter roughly the same shape but several inches larger in circumference than the container, holding securely, and shake once. The salad should unmold easily. Garnish the platter with the endive strips. Serve immediately.

NOTE: The salad can be made up to 1 day in advance.
Serves 6

Risi e Bisi Salad on Canadian Bacon and Fried Croutons

Risi e Bisi is the northern Italian specialty dish of rice and green peas. Here, the dish has been converted into a "new" salad, scoops of which crown little "rafts" of crunchy fried croutons and Canadian bacon. Serve the salad warm or at room temperature accompanied by dry white or red wine, if desired.

2 tablespoons lightly salted butter
2 tablespoons minced shallot
1¾ cups chicken broth
¼ cup dry white wine
1 cup raw long-grain rice
¼ teaspoon dried thyme
1¼ cups fresh green peas, cooked and drained, or one 10-ounce package frozen green peas, cooked and drained
½ cup black olive slivers
¼ cup diced seeded tomato
8 slices Canadian bacon, sautéed

Fried Croutons:

8 slices firm white bread
2 tablespoons sweet butter
2 tablespoons virgin olive oil

Heat the butter in a saucepan and cook the shallots for 3 minutes, stirring often. Add the chicken broth and white wine and bring to a boil. Stir in the rice, cover, and simmer for 20 minutes, or until the rice is tender and the liquid absorbed. Add the thyme, peas, olives, and tomato.

To make the fried croutons: Cut the bread slices into circles slightly larger than the diameter of the Canadian bacon. Heat the sweet butter and oil in a frying pan and cook the bread slices on each side, in batches, until golden brown.

For each salad, put two of the fried croutons on a dinner plate, top each with a slice of the bacon, then top each with a scoop of the salad.

Serves 4

Rice and Black Bean Salad with Sautéed Bananas

Rice and black beans are a terrific pair any time. Here they are converted into a fragrant salad spiked with cilantro, oregano, and radishes and garnished with sautéed bananas—contrasting flavors that complement each other deliciously.

3 cups cold cooked long-grain rice (approximately 1¼ cups uncooked)
2 cups cooked (1 cup uncooked dried) or canned black beans, rinsed and drained
1 14-ounce can baby corn, drained

2 tablespoons freshly chopped cilantro
   (coriander)
½ cup minced red radish
¼ cup diced white onion
3 tablespoons butter
4 medium-sized ripe but firm bananas, peeled
   and cut into ½-inch lengths on the diagonal

Bean Salad Dressing:

4 tablespoons red wine vinegar
1 garlic clove, minced
½ teaspoon dried oregano
¾ cup olive oil
Salt and freshly ground pepper to taste

Combine all the salad ingredients except for the butter and the bananas in a large bowl.

Make the dressing: Whisk together the vinegar, garlic, and oregano; drop by drop whisk in the oil; then season to taste with salt and pepper.

Pour the dressing over the salad and toss until well mixed.

Heat the butter in a large frying pan and cook the banana pieces quickly, in batches, over medium-high heat until lightly browned on each side.

Heap the salad onto a serving dish and garnish the edges with the banana slices immediately.

Serves 4

VEGETABLE SALADS

Wonderful main course vegetable salads are featured everywhere today. At home I get repeated requests for vegetable salads, especially for Vegetable Salad Pizzas (page 103), a refreshing and satisfying meal-in-one dish (I take it as a compliment that a teenage friend of mine refers to it as "funky salad"). Occasionally I'll add shrimp, anchovies, or cooked crumbled sausage or ground beef to the vegetable mixture topping for a palate-pleasing change of pace.

From coffee shops to elegant restaurants, salad lovers and the health-conscious seek out seasonal vegetable salad specials on menus. And one has only to take a look at the collection of beautifully displayed vegetable salads in the hundreds of takeout food shops around the country to see just how tempting and popular they are.

Vegetables have become delicious replacements for the traditional greens as a salad base, particularly in main course salads. Fabulous greens aren't excluded, though; they are often imaginatively included in vegetable salads, intensifying the color, texture, and flavor.

The cornucopia of vegetables available today enables us to create an amazing variety of vegetable salads. For example, a salad composed of julienne strips of crisp cooked zucchini, asparagus, leek, carrots, cucumbers, and beets tossed with arugula leaves, shredded romaine lettuce, and red cabbage and combined in an aromatic blend of lemon juice, white wine vinegar, extra-virgin olive oil, and herbs, topped with a sprinkling of butter-fried bread crumbs, pleases all the senses, and makes a light healthful meal as well.

Vegetables in a main course salad can be raw, blanched, or cooked to a crisp *al dente*. A combination of raw and cooked vegetables offers interesting textures—the silky bite of raw sliced mushrooms along with firm fleshy poached asparagus pieces tossed in a spicy red onion and blue cheese vinaigrette and served on a plate of fragrant sautéed bell peppers, sprinkled with crisp cooked bacon (page 101) is another delicious vegetable salad meal.

Vegetable salads needn't, of course, be limited to strict vegetarian fare; strips, slices, or cubes of cooked roast beef, poultry, lamb, pork, ham sausage, mortadella and other cold cuts, cooked eggs, and many types of cheeses add substance as well as complementing flavors and textures to main course vegetable salads. Beyond these additions, to nutritionally balance vegetable salads, mar-velous extras can be served, such as canapés of smoked salmon (page 108), or tasty small finger sandwiches: roast beef and watercress with horseradish and mayonnaise spread; curried egg salad with fresh basil leaves; or ham and brie with butter on the bread of your choice.

Vegetables can be cut into numerous shapes—sliced, diced, chopped, cubed, julienne, grated, shredded, or left whole; their individual shape and size add to the variety. One of my favorite salads, Technicolor Vegetable Salad, which follows, is an example.

Whichever salad or combination of vegetables you use, always select the season's very best offerings. They'll taste best, and cost less, too.

Whether from our own vegetable patch, a farmer's market, a quality greengrocer, or a supermarket's produce department, we are now able to choose from an abundant assortment of fresh vegetables to create a limitless variety of main course vegetable salads.

RECIPES

Asparagus, Mushroom, and Pepper Salad with Spicy Red Onion
and Blue Cheese Vinaigrette

Technicolor Vegetable Salad

Vegetable Salad Pizzas

Mixed Vegetables in Prosciutto

Vegetable Salad with Aioli Sauce

Gazpacho Salad

Tomato Aspic Ring with Gazpacho Salad

Mixed Vegetable and Lettuce Salad with Smoked Salmon Canapés

Asparagus, Mushroom, and Pepper Salad with Spicy Red Onion and Blue Cheese Vinaigrette

*H*ere's a robust vegetable salad crowned with bacon. Vegetarians can replace the bacon with oven-baked croutons (page 106). I serve garlic bread and dry red wine with this salad.

> 3 tablespoons virgin olive oil
> 4 large red bell peppers, cored and seeded, cut into 1-inch square pieces
> 1¼ pounds fresh asparagus, stem ends cut off, peeled, cut into 1-inch lengths on the diagonal*
> 12 ounces raw mushrooms, very thinly sliced
> 12 strips crisp cooked bacon, crumbled

Spicy Red Onion Vinaigrette:

> ½ cup diced red onion
> 1 tablespoon balsamic vinegar
> 2 tablespoons white wine vinegar
> 1 tablespoon Dijon mustard
> ½ teaspoon curry powder
> ¼ teaspoon dried thyme
> 1 cup virgin olive oil
> ⅓ cup crumbled blue cheese
> Salt and freshly ground pepper to taste

Prepare the vinaigrette first by combining the red onion, vinegars, mustard, curry powder, and thyme in a bowl. Drop by drop whisk in the oil. Add the cheese, mix and season to taste with salt and pepper. Set aside.

Heat the oil in a large frying pan and cook the peppers over medium-high heat for 5 minutes, turning often. Drain on paper towels.

Poach the asparagus in barely simmering lightly salted water in a saucepan for 6 minutes, or just until tender, but still crisp. Drain well and cool.

Arrange equal amounts of the peppers over the bottom of four dinner plates.

Combine the asparagus and mushrooms in a bowl and pour the dressing over them. Toss well. Spoon equal amounts of the mixture over the peppers on each plate. Sprinkle the tops of the salads equally with the bacon, and serve immediately.

Serves 4

* To peel asparagus, use a vegetable peeler and peel off the layer of green outer skin from just under the asparagus tips to the cut-off stem ends.

Technicolor Vegetable Salad

The vegetables starring in this beautiful salad combine contrasting, yet complementing colors, flavors, and textures. There is no dressing to speak of. The vegetables are only lightly moistened and coated with a mixture of olive oil and soy sauce.

For a recent luncheon, I served this salad accompanied by warm biscuits filled with baked ham and spread with goat cheese and honey, with goblets of iced tea garnished with mint sprigs, and a dessert of cold poached pears and sugar cookies. (The pears were cooked the night before and refrigerated until served. The cookies came from a favorite local bakery.)

Since the salad can rest at room temperature for one hour before being tossed and served, only the biscuits need to be prepared, cooked, and assembled just before dining. If time is a consideration, use crackers instead of biscuits. Spread the crackers with goat cheese and top with a slice of ham, then drizzle a little honey over the ham. (Vegetarians can eliminate the ham, of course.)

2 pounds small unpeeled new potatoes
3 tablespoons butter

3 tablespoons peanut or vegetable oil
Salt
1 10-ounce package frozen baby lima beans
1 pound French green beans, ends trimmed (or use regular-sized green beans, stringed and ends trimmed, cut into 1-inch lengths)
1 pound carrots, peeled and cut into julienne strips
1½ cups fresh corn (cut off cob)
1 pound unpeeled zucchini, diced
1 pound snow pea pods, stringed and stemmed
1 pint small yellow or red cherry tomatoes
½ cup thinly sliced scallion
¾ cup thinly sliced canned water chestnuts
2 tablespoons fresh chopped parsley
1 tablespoon fresh chopped basil (don't use dried)
1 tablespoon soy sauce
½ cup virgin olive oil
Salt and freshly ground pepper

Cook the potatoes covered in boiling water for about 10 to 12 minutes, or until just barely tender. Drain. Slice the potatoes in half if small; quarter ones larger than 1½ inches in diameter. Set aside.

Heat the butter and peanut or vegetable oil in a large frying pan and sauté the potatoes until the white sides are golden brown. Drain on paper towels.

Cook the lima beans according to the package directions, or just until tender, and drain. Put them in a large shallow bowl.

Bring 1½ quarts of water to a boil in a 3½- to 4½-quart saucepan. Add 1 teaspoon of salt. Cook the green beans for 3 minutes and remove them with a slotted spoon. Add the beans to the bowl with the lima beans. Now add the carrots, corn, and zucchini to the boiling water and cook them for 3 minutes. Transfer the cooked vegetables to the bowl with the beans, using a slotted spoon. Blanch the snow pea pods in the water for 30 seconds and drain well. Add them to the other vegetables along with the potatoes, tomatoes, scallion, water chestnuts, parsley, and basil and gently toss.

Whisk together the soy sauce and oil and drizzle over the vegetables and toss. Season to taste with salt and pepper.

Let the salad rest at least 15 minutes before serving it, then retoss. The vegetables can rest at room temperature for up to an hour, or can be covered and refrigerated for several hours. Retoss and serve cold or bring back to room temperature and retoss before serving.

Variation: One half a cup of toasted almonds can be tossed into the salad just before serving, if desired.

Serves 6

Vegetable Salad Pizzas

*T*hese fabulous vegetable salad pizzas are a meal in themselves and a vegetarian's delight. They are also a favorite with children who normally don't like vegetables.

1 cup finely chopped broccoli
1 cup finely chopped cauliflower flowerets
1 cup diced zucchini
8 frozen puff pastry pattie shells, thawed
1 cup marinara or tomato sauce
½ cup chopped onion
¾ cup diced tomato
¾ cup diced cored and seeded green bell pepper
1 teaspoon dried basil
1 teaspoon dried oregano
8 ounces grated mozzarella cheese
2 tablespoons freshly grated Parmesan cheese
Olive oil

Preheat the oven to 400°.

Blanch the broccoli, cauliflower, and zucchini as follows: Immerse the broccoli and cauliflower in simmering, lightly salted water for 3 minutes, the zucchini for 1 minute. Drain well.

To make the pizza shells: Stack two of the thawed pattie shells one on top of the other, roll them out to about 8 inches in diameter, and place on a lightly oiled baking sheet. Repeat for the three remaining pizza shells. (Two baking sheets are usually required.)

Spoon 4 tablespoons of the marinara sauce on top of each pizza shell and spread evenly over the surface to within a ½ inch of the edge of the shell.

Combine the blanched and raw vegetables and arrange evenly over the sauce.

Combine the basil, oregano, and cheeses and sprinkle equally over the vegetables.

Drizzle each pizza with a little olive oil and bake on the middle shelf of the oven for about 20 minutes or until golden brown.

Serves 4

Mixed Vegetables in Prosciutto

Serve finger sandwiches of Italian bread or rolls, thinly sliced tomato, fresh basil leaves, and butter with this delectable salad—a delicious combination of vegetables partially wrapped in prosciutto.

1 pound thinly sliced prosciutto, at room temperature

1 bunch arugula leaves, washed, dried, and stemmed
1 small cucumber, peeled and seeded, halved, and thinly sliced
¾ cup minced jarred roasted red peppers, well drained and patted dry
¾ cup very thinly, diagonally sliced celery hearts
1 cup bean sprouts
1 cup thinly sliced mushrooms

Balsamic Vinaigrette II:

2 tablespoons balsamic vinegar
1 teaspoon Dijon mustard
½ teaspoon minced garlic
½ cup virgin olive oil
Salt and freshly ground pepper to taste

Make the dressing first: Whisk together the vinegar, mustard, and garlic in a bowl; drop by drop whisk in the oil; and season to taste with salt and pepper.

Arrange overlapping layers of the prosciutto to completely line each of four dinner plates.

Combine the salad ingredients and toss in the dressing. Place equal portions of the salad in the center of the prosciutto and bring the edges of the prosciutto up over the salad, covering it by half. Serve immediately.

Serves 4

Vegetable Salad with Aioli Sauce

*E*lizabeth David, the respected English food writer, describes aioli in her extraordinary volume *French Provincial Cooking* as, "The magnificent shining golden ointment" or "butter of Provence." The creamy garlic-infused mayonnaise is the perfect foil for fresh cooked and raw vegetables.

Serve with plenty of *pain grillé* (grilled bread). To make it, grill slices of French bread over the barbecue or toast under the broiler.

    4 hard-boiled eggs, peeled and halved
    8 new potatoes, cooked and sliced
    ½ pound cooked fresh French or regular green
        beans
    1 10-ounce package frozen artichoke hearts,
        cooked and drained
    ½ pound carrots, peeled, sliced, and cooked
    4 stalks celery, cut into sticks
    1 red bell pepper, cored, seeded, and cut into
        rings
    1 yellow bell pepper, cored, seeded, and cut into
        rings
    8 red radishes, trimmed

Aioli Sauce:

    2 teaspoons minced garlic
    Generous pinch of ground saffron
    3 large egg yolks, at room temperature
    1½ cups virgin olive oil
    2 teaspoons freshly squeezed lemon juice
    Salt to taste
    Freshly ground pepper

Arrange hard-boiled egg halves and the cooked and raw vegetables on a large serving platter.

To make the aioli sauce: Mash the garlic with the saffron until a very smooth puree-paste is formed. Whisk the egg yolks thoroughly with the garlic paste. Drop by drop whisk in the oil, then season lightly with the lemon juice and salt to taste.

Turn the sauce into a bowl and serve with the salad. Pass the peppermill.

Serves 4

Gazpacho Salad

*T*his meal-in-one salad has become one of my favorite diet meals. The crunchy textures of the vegetables and croutons give it substance, and the tart dressing includes only four tablespoons of olive oil, keeping the calorie count low. Each serving of Gazpacho Salad is under 300 calories.

For a variation, serve the salad in the center of a tomato aspic ring (see below).

1 cup diced cored and seeded red, yellow, or green bell pepper (or a combination)
1 medium-sized cucumber, peeled and cut into ½-inch cubes
1 cup diced celery
½ cup chopped red onion
2 cups diced firm but ripe seeded tomato
1 cup raw unpeeled zucchini, cut into ½-inch cubes
½ cup diced radish
4 tablespoons red wine vinegar
4 tablespoons virgin olive oil
¾ cup V-8 juice, chilled
Salt and freshly ground pepper to taste
4 large leaves romaine lettuce, washed and dried
2 hard-boiled eggs, coarsely chopped (optional)

Oven-Baked Croutons:

4 slices day-old firm white bread, cut into ½-inch cubes

Preheat the oven to 350°.
Put the vegetables into a large bowl and combine gently.
Combine the vinegar, oil, and V-8 juice in a bowl, pour over the vegetables, and toss. Season to taste lightly with salt and pepper. Cover and refrigerate.

Make the croutons: Spread the bread cubes over a baking sheet and bake for about 10 to 12 minutes until they are golden brown, stirring and turning after 5 minutes. Cool.

Toss the salad again. Put one romaine lettuce leaf on each of four dinner plates. Spoon equal amounts of the salad over the lettuce and garnish with the chopped eggs and croutons.
Serves 4

Tomato Aspic Ring with Gazpacho Salad

All this savory salad needs is a few crisp crackers as an accompaniment. Keep in mind that most chicken salads can deliciously replace the Gazpacho Salad in this recipe. To serve eight to ten, double the recipes and use a 2-quart ring mold.

2 envelopes unflavored gelatin
¼ cup cold water
4 cups tomato juice

1 teaspoon tomato juice
1 teaspoon Worcestershire sauce
½ teaspoon celery salt
1 tablespoon chopped fresh parsley
1 teaspoon sugar
1 recipe Gazpacho Salad (page 106)

Soften the gelatin in the cold water.

Meanwhile, heat 2 cups of the tomato juice in a saucepan. Remove from heat, stir in the softened gelatin, and stir until dissolved.

Add the remaining tomato juice and the rest of the aspic ingredients. Pour into a 1-quart ring mold and chill until firm.

To unmold: Lower the mold carefully into a basin of hot water for 5 seconds. Place a large serving plate on top of the mold and, holding the plate and mold securely, invert and give one good shake. The aspic should unmold easily.

Fill the center of the ring with half the Gazpacho Salad and surround the outer edges of the ring with the remaining salad. Garnish with the croutons and eggs.

Serves 4 to 6

Mixed Vegetable and Lettuce Salad with Smoked Salmon Canapés

The colors and textures of this glorious vegetable salad make me think of a Matisse painting. Pungent little canapés of smoked salmon pureed with crème fraîche, a touch of lemon juice, cayenne pepper, and scallions spread on toasted French bread and showered with freshly ground pepper accent this vegetable salad beautifully. Serve with iced tea, each glass garnished with a slice of fresh lime.

1 dozen small hearts of romaine lettuce leaves, separated, washed, and dried
3 small Belgian endive, stemmed, leaves separated
1 small bunch watercress, washed, dried, and stems trimmed
Salt
3 cups water
¼ pound snow pea pods, stems and strings removed
16 baby carrots, peeled and left whole, with ¾-inch of the stem tops intact

6 unpeeled baby zucchini, cut lengthwise into
⅛-inch-thick slices
8 asparagus spears
1 small red bell pepper, cored, seeded, and cut
lengthwise into thin julienne strips
½ pint tiny yellow pear-shaped tomatoes or
tiny red cherry tomatoes
½ cup thinly sliced black olives
⅔ cup very thinly sliced celery hearts, cut on
the diagonal

Lime Vinaigrette:

2 tablespoons freshly squeezed lime juice
2 tablespoons champagne or white wine vinegar
2 teaspoons grated onion
½ teaspoon dry mustard
½ cup virgin olive oil
Salt and freshly ground pepper to taste

Put the lettuce, endive, and watercress
into a bowl and refrigerate while preparing
the rest of the salad.

Lightly salt the water, bring to a boil, and
briefly cook the pea pods, carrots, zucchini,
and asparagus separately as follows: Cook
the snow peas 1 minute, the carrots 4 minutes, the zucchini 1 minute, and the asparagus 5 minutes. After cooking each
vegetable, remove from saucepan and cool
under cold water to refresh, and drain well.
After refreshing and draining the asparagus,
cut each stalk in half lengthwise.

Put all of the vegetables in a large bowl
and gently combine. Cover and refrigerate.

To make the vinaigrette, whisk together
the lime juice, vinegar, onion, and dry mustard; drop by drop whisk in the oil; then
season to taste with salt and pepper.

Pour one-third of the dressing over the
combined greens and toss. Arrange the
greens over the bottom of a large shallow
salad or serving bowl.

Pour the remaining vinaigrette over the
vegetables and gently toss.

Spoon the mixed vegetables over the lettuce and serve with the canapés.
Serves 4

Smoked Salmon Canapés

3 ounces smoked salmon, coarsely chopped
½ cup crème fraîche (page 76)
2 teaspoons freshly squeezed lemon juice
1 or 2 dashes of cayenne pepper
1 tablespoon chopped scallion
12 ½-inch-thick slices French bread
Freshly ground black pepper

Puree the smoked salmon, crème fraîche,
lemon juice, cayenne pepper, and scallion
well in the food processor.

Lightly toast both sides of the slices of
bread and cool.

Just before serving, spread the salmon puree evenly over the toast slices and grate black pepper over the top of each.

The smoked salmon spread can be prepared one day ahead and kept covered in the refrigerator.

Makes 12 canapes

BEEF AND VEAL SALADS

Recently a friend of mine returned from Paris, and we met for lunch so that she could recount the highlights of her trip. This is an anticipated ritual that we always plan after either one of us takes a trip abroad. It's part of the fun of returning home and of being a dedicated mental traveler. At the top of the list of experiences to cover is always food. My friend sat down and said, "Beef Vinaigrette."

She and her husband had been having exceptional, but filling, four- or five-course meals for several days, so one day they agreed to lunch at *any* small neighborhood restaurant that they could find after visiting an art exhibit. They also planned to order just one dish no matter how unhappy it made the waiter.

The beef vinaigrette that they ordered turned out to be the most memorable dish of their entire stay in Paris. Thin strips of tender rare fillet of beef were tossed in a sharp mustard vinaigrette dressing with bits of red onion and chopped parsley. They ate a basket of crusty French bread to soak up the fabulous dressing, drank a bottle of red Burgundy, and couldn't resist a sensational apple tart with crème fraîche for dessert.

Beef and veal do make great main course salads, and they are excellent choices for entertaining. It is interesting to observe that when a beef or veal main course salad is served at a dinner party, there is usually never any left over.

Many cuts of cooked beef can be utilized in main course salads: broiled or grilled flank steak, strips of sirloin or roast beef, and, of course, fillet.

Because veal is so expensive, it might be considered extravagant to purchase a boneless veal roast to make a salad. But we buy costly lobster for salad-making, so why not veal? Veal always makes an elegant entrée.

Italy's renowned *vitello tonnato*, a magnificent dish of thinly sliced roast veal with a creamy sauce of canned tunafish, olive oil, anchovies, and lemon juice can be turned into a superb main course salad. The veal, cut into strips or cubes and tossed in the same sauce lightened with extra olive oil, is served on a bed of crisp greens with cherry tomatoes and Greek black olives.

Beef and veal lend themselves to a wide variety of dressings from Chinese sweet and sour, herbed mayonnaise, or Caesar-style dressing to Roquefort dressing or a mustard vinaigrette.

Keep in mind, too, that beef and veal are interchangeable in many recipes.

ECIPES

Marinated Beef, Red Onion, and Yellow Pepper Kebab Salad
Roast Beef, Cauliflower, and Walnut Salad with Roquefort Dressing
Beef Vinaigrette Salad
Deli Tongue Salad
Brisket and Carrot Salad on a Chiffonade of Greens
Curried Beef Salad
Thai Beef and Vegetable Salad
Reuben's Salad
Veal and Mushroom Salad with Pink Tartar Sauce Dressing
Veal and Cherry Tomato Salad with Mustard-Caper Dressing

Marinated Beef, Red Onion, and Yellow Pepper Kebab Salad

As often happens in the world of food and cooking, discoveries are made by happenstance. In this case, two leftover cooked kebabs were turned into a salad so satisfying that now I cook the kebabs in order to prepare the salad. The only change I make is to cook the red onions and yellow peppers separately. The Salsa Verde Mayonnaise affords a pungent flavor contrast.

This salad also makes a delicious sandwich on French or Italian bread.

1½ pounds flank steak, cut against the grain into ⅛-inch-thick slices, each slice cut into lengths about 1½ inches long
3 tablespoons peanut or vegetable oil
2 medium-sized red onions, cut into slivers
2 large yellow bell peppers, cored, seeded, and cut into ¼-inch-thick slices
Salt and freshly ground pepper to taste

Kebab Marinade:

½ cup peanut or vegetable oil
⅓ cup Oriental sesame oil
½ cup soy sauce
½ cup dry sherry
1 tablespoon Worcestershire sauce
½ cup brown sugar (packed)
1 teaspoon minced garlic

Salsa Verde Mayonnaise:

½ cup coarsely chopped washed and dried watercress
¼ cup coarsely chopped fresh parsley
6 fresh basil leaves
1 cup mayonnaise or Classic Mayonnaise (page 128)
1 or 2 dashes of Tabasco sauce or other hot sauce
Salt and freshly ground pepper to taste

Combine the marinade ingredients in a large bowl. Add the beef slices, toss, cover, and refrigerate overnight or at least 3 hours.

Make the dressing: Finely chop the watercress, parsley, and basil in a food processor. Add the mayonnaise and Tabasco sauce and puree until very smooth. Season to taste with salt and pepper, cover, and refrigerate until used.

Heat the outdoor grill or oven broiler.

Soak four 8-inch wooden skewers for 30 minutes. Drain the meat (reserving the marinade) and thread it onto the skewers in equal amounts. The meat slices should fit snugly together on each skewer. Grill or broil the meat about 5 minutes per side.

Meanwhile, strain the marinade, bring to a boil in a small saucepan, and cook for 3 minutes. Baste the kebabs with the marinade after turning them over.

Cool the kebabs.

Heat the oil in a large frying pan and cook the onions and pepper over high heat, stir-frying them for about 4 minutes until golden brown. Season them to taste with salt and pepper.

Transfer the onions and peppers to a large salad bowl and add the beef from the kebabs and 3 tablespoons of the marinade. Toss well.

Serve the salad at room temperature or cold with the Salsa Verde Mayonnaise and crusty French or Italian bread.

Serves 4

Roast Beef, Cauliflower, and Walnut Salad with Roquefort Dressing

*T*his practically instant hearty salad is a great blend of distinct flavors. If desired, serve with fresh cooked asparagus.

1½ pounds medium-rare roast beef, cut into ⅛-inch slices
3 cups thinly sliced raw cauliflower flowerets
1 tablespoon chopped fresh parsley
⅓ cup chopped walnuts

Roquefort Dressing:

3 tablespoons white wine vinegar
1 tablespoon Dijon mustard
1 teaspoon Worcestershire sauce
2 tablespoons walnut oil
¼ cup virgin olive oil
½ cup vegetable oil
3 ounces crumbled Roquefort cheese
Salt and freshly ground pepper to taste

Cut the roast beef slices into ¼-inch-thick strips and combine with the cauliflower in a bowl.

To make the dressing, whisk together the vinegar, mustard, and Worcestershire sauce, then drop by drop whisk in the oils, stir in the Roquefort cheese, and season to taste with salt and pepper.

Turn the dressing over the salad, toss well, and sprinkle with the parsley and walnuts. Serve immediately, or cover and chill for several hours. If chilling, don't add parsley or walnuts until just before serving.

Serves 4

Beef Vinaigrette Salad

*T*his straightforward salad of tender fillet of beef in a robust vinaigrette dressing makes a very special main course salad that can easily be doubled. Accompanied with a side dish of cooked sugar snap peas or green beans, French bread and butter, and a red wine, it makes a very memorable meal.

2 pounds cooked fillet of beef, cooked medium-
    rare, cut into strips 1 inch by 2 inches
2 tablespoons chopped fresh parsley

Sharp Mustard Vinaigrette:

3 tablespoons red wine vinegar
2 tablespoons Dijon mustard
¼ cup diced red onion
¾ cup virgin olive oil
Salt and freshly ground pepper to taste

Make the dressing: Whisk together the vinegar, mustard, and red onion; drop by drop whisk in the oil; then season well with salt and pepper to taste.

Pour the mixture over the beef slices in a large bowl, add the parsley, and toss. Serve at room temperature or chilled after one or two hours' refrigeration.

Serves 4

Deli Tongue Salad

*O*ur families' food preferences play an important role in meal-planning. My husband's affinity for tongue inspired this recipe. Serve the salad with black or rye bread, sweet butter, and thick slices of tomato and red onion.

3 cups cooked tongue cut into julienne strips
¾ cup very thinly sliced celery
¼ cup very thinly sliced red radish
1 tablespoon chopped fresh parsley
Salt and freshly ground pepper to taste
4 large sour pickles

Spicy Dressing:

¾ cup mayonnaise or Classic Mayonnaise
    (page 128)
1 tablespoon chili sauce
1 tablespoon Dusseldorf mustard
⅛ teaspoon curry powder
1 teaspoon honey

Combine the tongue, celery, radish, and parsley in a bowl.

Blend the dressing ingredients together in a small bowl. Turn the mixture over the salad ingredients, and combine. Season to taste with salt and pepper.

Slice the pickles into ⅛-inch slices, and make a circular border with equal amounts of them on each of four dinner plates. Spoon the salad into the center of each plate in equal portions and serve. Or cover and chill salad for several hours and serve cold.

Serves 4

Brisket and Carrot Salad on a Chiffonade of Greens

This substantial and piquant salad is great for a winter family dinner, and it's also a crowd-pleaser. Like so many main course salads, it can easily be doubled or tripled. The tangy Dill-Mustard Vinaigrette dressing is extremely versatile; shrimp, chicken, lamb, or pork can be substituted for the brisket in the recipe in the same quantity with excellent results. Or use the dressing on any combination of mixed greens and/ or vegetables, for about 1½ quarts of salad.

Serve with hot or warm buttered biscuits.

3½ cups cooked brisket or boiled beef, thinly
   sliced and cut into ½-inch strips
2 cups cooked thinly sliced peeled carrots

1 cup thinly shredded washed and dried
   romaine lettuce
1½ cups thinly shredded iceberg lettuce

Dill-Mustard Vinaigrette:

1 egg yolk, at room temperature
1 tablespoon Dijon mustard
¼ cup red wine vinegar
2 minced shallots
¾ cup virgin olive oil
1 tablespoon chopped fresh dill, or 1 teaspoon
   dried dill
Salt and freshly ground pepper to taste

Combine the beef and carrots in a large bowl.

Make the dressing: Whisk together the egg yolk, mustard, vinegar, and shallots in a small bowl. Drop by drop whisk in the oil. Add the dill and season to taste with salt and pepper.

Pour the dressing over the beef and carrots and combine thoroughly. Serve immediately, or cover and thoroughly chill and serve at room temperature. Toss before serving.

Serve the individual salads on beds of the combined lettuces.

Serves 4

Curried Beef Salad

*H*ere is yet another first-rate salad that uses leftovers beautifully, *and* the salad works equally well substituting cooked lamb or pork for the beef. Serve on a bed of bean sprouts or a chiffonade of romaine or iceberg lettuce, garnished with cherry tomatoes, if desired. Serve sliced toasted brioche with the salad.

3½ cups cubed cooked fillet, sirloin, or roast beef
½ cup diced seedless cucumber
½ cup diced celery
½ cup diced cored and seeded yellow, red, or green bell pepper
¼ cup thinly sliced scallion
1 tablespoon chopped fresh parsley
1 cup mango chutney

Curried Mayonnaise III:

1 cup mayonnaise or Classic Mayonnaise (page 128)
¼ cup sour cream
1 tablespoon curry powder
½ teaspoon turmeric
1 tablespoon freshly squeezed lemon juice

Put the beef, cucumber, celery, pepper, and scallions into a large bowl.

Combine the dressing ingredients in a small bowl, turn the mixture over the salad, and combine well.

Sprinkle the salad with the parsley just before serving and pass the chutney. Serve at room temperature or cover and chill for several hours and serve cold.

Serves 4

Thai Beef and Vegetable Salad

*H*ere is a remarkably good salad. The beef marinates for at least three hours to bring out all the combined flavors of the sauce, especially the lime and cilantro, and the vegetables are added just before serving. Serve with cooked rice at room temperature.

1 pound lean flank steak
Vegetable oil
1 cup chopped fresh cauliflower
1 small cucumber, peeled, halved lengthwise, seeded, and diced
1 medium-sized firm ripe tomato, seeded and diced
½ cup diced cored and seeded red bell pepper
¼ cup thinly sliced scallion

Thai Sauce:

¾ cup freshly squeezed lime juice
2 tablespoons Oriental sesame oil
½ cup fish sauce*
½ cup finely chopped fresh cilantro (coriander)
2 teaspoons minced garlic
Pinch of hot pepper flakes
Freshly ground pepper to taste

Brush the beef lightly with oil and grill or broil for 10 minutes per side. Cool.

Meanwhile, combine the sauce ingredients in a large bowl.

Cut the meat into very thin slices, against the grain, on the diagonal. Add the meat to the sauce, mix, cover, and refrigerate for at least 3 hours. (The salad can marinate for up to 8 hours.) Serve at room temperature.

Add the vegetables to the beef and sauce, combine, and serve.

Serves 4

* Available bottled in Oriental or specialty food stores.

Reuben's Salad

The famous Reuben's sandwich, turned salad, was tested one day when we had all the ingredients to put together the sandwich except the rye bread. The salad was such a success that it's become a favorite in our house. We now serve the rye bread with butter on the side.

1 pound sliced corned beef, cut into
    ¼-inch-thick strips crosswise
¾ pound sliced Muenster cheese, cut into
    ¼-inch-thick strips crosswise
8 ounces sauerkraut, well-drained
1 small head romaine lettuce, washed, dried,
    and torn into bite-sized pieces
1 medium-sized red onion, thinly sliced and
    separated into rings

Russian Dressing:

1 cup mayonnaise or Classic Mayonnaise
    (page 128)
¼ cup chili sauce
¼ cup diced sweet gherkin pickles
½ teaspoon caraway seed
1 teaspoon freshly squeezed lemon juice

Put the corned beef, cheese, and sauerkraut into a large bowl.

Combine the dressing ingredients in a small bowl, turn over the salad, and toss well.

Arrange the romaine on the bottom of a shallow serving dish, top with the salad, and garnish the top of the salad with the onion rings.

Serves 4

Veal and Mushroom Salad with Pink Tartar Sauce Dressing

*T*his remarkably easy, delicious salad is the result of leftover veal from preparation of a *vitello tonnato*. The veal can be replaced with chicken, lamb, or pork. For summer you might begin a meal featuring this salad with a cold cream of celery soup; in winter, a hot cream of celery soup. Dessert for a summer menu might be an apple tart à la mode, and for a warming winter's dessert, hot apple pie with warm cream.

    3 cups diced cooked veal
    10 ounces thinly sliced mushrooms
    2 tablespoons chopped fresh parsley
    3 cups washed dried and torn mixed greens
        such as romaine lettuce, spinach, and
        chicory

Pink Tartar Sauce Dressing:

    1 cup mayonnaise or Classic Mayonnaise
        (page 128)
    2 tablespoons white wine vinegar
    1 teaspoon Dijon mustard
    2 tablespoons ketchup
    2 tablespoons drained capers

    2 tablespoons minced cornichon pickles
    2 tablespoons minced shallot
    Salt and freshly ground pepper to taste

Combine the tartar sauce ingredients in a large bowl.

Add the veal, mushrooms, and parsley, toss well, and serve on mixed greens, if desired.

Serves 4

Veal and Cherry Tomato Salad with Mustard-Caper Dressing

*F*or this attractive and elegant salad, strips of cooked veal scallops are arranged in a single row, topped with cherry tomatoes that have been tossed in a tart mustard-caper dressing. Serve with toasted pita bread and sweet butter.

    1½ pounds veal scallops, pounded flat to
        ⅛-inch thickness between 2 sheets of wax
        paper

Salt and freshly ground pepper
3 tablespoons butter
2 tablespoons peanut or vegetable oil
1 pint cherry tomatoes, halved
1 tablespoon chopped fresh parsley

Mustard-Caper Dressing:

1 tablespoon balsamic vinegar
3 tablespoons red wine vinegar
1 tablespoon Dijon mustard
½ cup olive oil
2 tablespoons capers
Salt and freshly ground pepper to taste

Pat the veal dry and season it lightly with salt and pepper.

Heat 1½ tablespoons of the butter with the oil in a large frying pan and cook the veal in batches over medium-high heat for about 3 minutes per side. Add the remaining butter as needed.

Drain the veal on paper towels. Cool.

To make the dressing, whisk together the vinegars and mustard; drop by drop whisk in the oil; stir in the capers, and season with salt and pepper to taste.

Cut the veal into ¼-inch-thick strips and arrange on a rectangular-shaped serving dish in one long row. (If you don't have a rectangular dish, use an oval one.)

Combine the cherry tomatoes, dressing, and parsley in a bowl and toss. Spoon the mixture over the veal and serve immediately.

Serves 4

POULTRY SALADS

Poultry salads are universally appreciated as delicious, healthful, economical, and incredibly versatile.

A first-rate plain chicken salad, a composition of tender chicken and top-quality mayonnaise, is a small wonder in itself. From this simple, elegant combination, scores of salads can be created, as you will see by the recipes in this chapter.

As a teenager, one of the first chicken salads that I experimented with was a BLT chicken salad. I combined diced chicken with crumbled bacon, diced tomatoes, and shredded iceberg lettuce with mayonnaise, and seasoned it to taste with salt and pepper. It couldn't have been simpler or better.

Grilled, broiled, poached, roast, and even fried chicken make great chicken salads. The various cooking methods impart different flavors and textures to salads, of course. Breaded strips of chicken breast, fried to crispness, well-drained, and placed on top of mixed greens, drizzled with an herb vinaigrette dressing, make an unusually delectable main course chicken salad. Tender poached chicken cubes, cucumber, and beets, combined in a creamy dill and horseradish dressing served with rye toast points create a Russian-style main course.

The list of possibilities is virtually endless. In a master recipe notebook that I keep, there are over two hundred entries listed under chicken salads. Here I begin with Classic Chicken Salad and follow it with some of my favorite quick-and-easy chicken salads, then ten more main course chicken salads that I've collected over the years. Because so many chicken salad recipes call for mayonnaise and because the quality of the mayonnaise can make such a difference in a chicken salad, I also include my favorite mayonnaise recipe.

Turkey, with its own unique flavor, offers a lovely alternative to chicken in salad-making. It can be substituted for chicken in most chicken salad recipes, which enables us to use up leftover turkey. When entertaining a crowd, roasting a whole turkey or a large turkey breast for the salad instead of cooking batches of chicken, provides plenty of succulent white and dark meat, and is economical in money and time.

On the other hand, chicken can be substituted in turkey salad recipes if you like.

Duck salads make great company meals. A duck breast, sautéed and thinly sliced, topped with a complementing, contrasting dressing, is cause for celebration. And, tender duck meat can be combined with chicken or turkey, which extends the duck and produces an interesting mixture.

Cornish game hens have also become great vehicles for new salad-making, because of their lean, tender meat, and they are perfectly portioned for one serving. Butterflied and roasted or grilled Cornish game hen set on top of crisp greens with a curried mayonnaise dressing or an oil-and-vinegar-based garlic and herb dressing makes a very special easy main course salad.

RECIPES

Classic Chicken Salad

Chicken Salad with Bacon and Pesto Sauce

Chicken Salad Amandine

Chicken Tonnato Salad

Green Goddess Chicken Salad

Curried Chicken Salad

Creamy Tarragon Chicken Salad

Greek Lemon Chicken Salad

Chicken and Walnut Salad with Endive and Snow Pea Pods

Cobb Salad

Polynesian Chicken and Fruit Salad with Bananas

Chicken and Celeriac Salad

Chicken and Sugar Snap Pea Salad

Barbecued Chicken and Baked Bean Salad on Toasted Corn Muffins

Grilled Chicken Breast and Sun-Dried Tomato Salad

(continued)

RECIPES

Chicken and Cucumber Salad with Dill
Peking Chicken Salad in Lettuce Cups
Lemon Chicken and Cilantro Salad
Curried Turkey and Wild Rice Salad
Smoked Turkey, Mozzarella, and Tomato Salad with Fried Capers
Turkey Hash Salad with Sour Cream Dressing
Turkey Salad Veronique in a Bread Bowl
Turkey and Cherry Tomato Salad with Mustard-Dill Dressing
Cornish Game Hen and Vegetable Salad
Warm Duck and Sauerkraut Salad with Raspberry Vinegar
Duck, Gruyère, and Endive Salad with Cantaloupe
Waldorf Salad with Duck and Red Currant Sauce

Classic Chicken Salad

Where chicken salad is concerned, purists usually only want a combination of the tenderest breast of chicken and good mayonnaise, seasoned lightly with salt and pepper. Other chicken salad lovers insist that dark meat, celery, parsley, and scallions really *make* chicken salad. It's all a matter of personal taste.

My favorite chicken salad is the purist's version, made with homemade mayonnaise plus a little lemon juice and green peas, a perfect combination and a meal-in-one dish. The following classic recipe is made with chicken breasts, but half the amount in dark meat can be substituted, five thighs instead of two of the chicken breasts. For the most flavorful, moist, and tender meat, the chicken is cooked and cooled in the chicken stock. It is necessary to cook the chicken with the skins and bones intact for the most flavor.

1½ quarts homemade chicken stock or
   canned chicken broth
2 carrots, peeled and sliced
2 celery stalks, sliced
1 onion, quartered
1 garlic clove, coarsely chopped
1 bay leaf
6 sprigs parsley
6 peppercorns
4 large chicken breasts with bones in, halved
1¼ cups fresh peas cooked and drained and
   chilled, or 1 10-ounce package frozen green
   peas, cooked and drained and chilled
   (optional)
¼ cup diced celery (optional)
2 thinly sliced scallions (optional)
1 cup Classic Mayonnaise (page 128) or
   quality commercial mayonnaise
2 teaspoons freshly squeezed lemon juice
Salt and freshly ground pepper to taste
2 teaspoons chopped fresh parsley

Put the chicken stock, carrots, celery, onion, garlic, bay leaf, parsley, and peppercorns into a 3½-quart saucepan and bring to a boil. Add the chicken, stir, and bring back to the boil. Immediately reduce the heat to a simmer and cook for exactly 20 minutes. Skim off the scum as it rises.

Remove the pan from the heat and allow the chicken to cool in the stock for 30 minutes. Remove the chicken, and drain the stock and save it for another use.

Skin and bone the chicken.

Cut the chicken into bite-sized cubes or strips and put it into a large bowl with the green peas, if used. Add the celery and/or scallions if desired.

Mix together the mayonnaise and lemon

juice, season to taste with salt and pepper, and turn over the chicken. Combine well.

Serve immediately or cover and refrigerate for several hours. Serve cold. Sprinkle with freshly chopped parsley just before serving.

Serves 4

Classic Mayonnaise

Homemade mayonnaise is superb and easily made. It is important that all the ingredients used be brought to room temperature before beginning. For the best flavor and consistency, freshly made mayonnaise should be used within an hour of its preparation. Classic Mayonnaise can be used instead of commercial mayonnaise in any salad recipe. This recipe is easily doubled.

1 large egg yolk, at room temperature
1 teaspoon lemon juice
½ teaspoon salt or to taste
½ cup olive oil
½ cup vegetable oil
½ teaspoon Dijon mustard (optional)
½ teaspoon white wine vinegar (optional)
Freshly ground white pepper to taste

Put the egg yolk into a bowl and combine with the lemon juice and salt with a wire whisk. Drop by drop whisk in the olive and vegetable oils. Add the mustard, white wine vinegar, and pepper and blend in thoroughly with the whisk. Taste for seasoning and use immediately, or cover and chill until used.

Makes about 1¼ cups

Chicken Salad with Bacon and Pesto Sauce

¼ cup packed fresh basil leaves
1 tablespoon chopped fresh parsley
1 garlic clove, chopped
1 tablespoon freshly squeezed lemon juice
¾ cup mayonnaise or Classic Mayonnaise (page 128)
Salt and freshly ground pepper to taste
3½ cups cooked chicken (page 127), cut into ¼-inch strips
10 crisp cooked bacon strips, crumbled

Put the basil, parsley, and garlic into the container of a food processor and chop fine. Add the lemon juice and mayonnaise and puree until very smooth. Season to taste with salt and pepper.

Combine the chicken and bacon in a large bowl, turn the dressing over them, and blend well. Serve immediately.

Serves 4

Chicken Salad Amandine

3 tablespoons butter
1 tablespoon peanut or vegetable oil
¾ cup sliced almonds
3½ cups shredded light and dark meat cooked chicken (page 127)
½ cup thinly sliced celery hearts
1 cup mayonnaise or Classic Mayonnaise (page 128)
2 tablespoons Grand Marnier (optional)
½ teaspoon curry powder
Salt and freshly ground pepper to taste

Heat the butter and oil in a large frying pan and cook the almond slices until golden brown. Drain.

Put the chicken, celery, and almonds into a large bowl.

Combine the remaining ingredients, turn over the chicken mixture, and mix well.

Spoon the salad into a salad bowl and serve immediately.

Serves 4

Chicken Tonnato Salad

3½ cups cubed cooked chicken breast (page 127)
1 6½-ounce can solid white-meat tuna, packed in oil, well-drained
1 cup mayonnaise or Classic Mayonnaise (page 128)
1 tablespoon freshly squeezed lemon juice
8 anchovy fillets, drained and chopped
½ cup virgin olive oil
3 tablespoons drained capers
Salt and freshly ground pepper to taste

Put the chicken into a large bowl.

Add the tuna, mayonnaise, lemon juice, and anchovies to the container of a food processor and blend. With the machine running, add the olive oil in a slow, steady stream through the feed tube.

Turn the mixture over the chicken, add the capers, and combine well. Season to taste with salt and pepper.

Serve at room temperature, or cover and chill thoroughly. Bring to room temperature and toss before serving.

Serves 4

Green Goddess Chicken Salad

3½ cups cooked chicken (page 127)
¾ cup mayonnaise or Classic Mayonnaise
    (page 128)
6 anchovy fillets, drained and finely chopped
1 tablespoon chopped fresh tarragon leaves, or
    1 teaspoon dried tarragon
1 tablespoon freshly squeezed lemon juice
2 tablespoons tarragon vinegar
2 scallions, white parts only, thinly sliced
Salt and freshly ground pepper

Put the chicken in a large bowl.

In a small bowl mix together the mayonnaise, anchovies, tarragon, lemon juice, vinegar, and scallions and combine well. Season to taste with salt and pepper.

Turn the dressing over the chicken and combine. Serve immediately, or cover and refrigerate. Serve cold.
Serves 4

Curried Chicken Salad

3½ cups shredded cooked chicken (page 127)
½ cup diced canned water chestnuts
¼ cup minced scallion
2 stalks celery, diced
1 cup mayonnaise or Classic Mayonnaise
    (page 128)
1 tablespoon freshly squeezed lemon juice
1 tablespoon curry powder
¼ teaspoon turmeric
Salt and freshly ground pepper to taste

Toss together the chicken, water chestnuts, scallions, and celery in a large bowl.

Combine the remaining ingredients in a small bowl, turn over the chicken mixture, and blend well. Cover and refrigerate for at least 1 hour before serving. Serve chilled.
Serves 4

Creamy Tarragon Chicken Salad

3½ cups cubed cooked chicken (page 127)
1¼ cups fresh green peas, cooked, drained, and
    chilled or 1 10-ounce package frozen green
    peas, cooked and drained (optional)

1 cup mayonnaise or Classic Mayonnaise
   (page 128)
2 tablespoons tarragon vinegar
1 tablespoon chopped fresh tarragon, or
   1 teaspoon dried tarragon
1 tablespoon minced fresh chives
Salt and freshly ground pepper to taste

Put the chicken in a large bowl and toss with the peas if used.

Combine the remaining ingredients in a small bowl and turn the mixture over the chicken and peas. Blend well. Cover and chill for at least 1 hour before serving.

Serves 4

Greek Lemon Chicken Salad

3½ cups cooked chicken (page 127), cut into
   bite-sized pieces
½ cup black Greek olive slivers
¼ cup diced red onion
1 cup mayonnaise or Classic Mayonnaise
   (page 128)
1 tablespoon freshly squeezed lemon juice
1 teaspoon freshly grated lemon rind
1 teaspoon dried oregano
Salt and freshly ground pepper to taste

Toss together the chicken, olives, and red onion in a large bowl.

Combine the remaining ingredients, turn over the chicken mixture, and blend well. Cover and refrigerate for at least 1 hour. Serve chilled and toss again before serving.

Serves 4

Chicken and Walnut Salad with Endive and Snow Pea Pods

This tasty walnut-oil-flavored chicken salad is great for any season of the year; the accompanying dishes can be changed in appreciation of a particular season. For example, a spring/summer menu could begin with a platter of sliced seasonal fruit. A fall/winter menu's first course might be hot Quiche Lorraine. Dessert in any season: a savory bread pudding.

3 large boned and skinned chicken breasts,
   halved and pounded flat to ¼-inch thickness
   between 2 sheets of wax paper
Salt and freshly ground pepper to taste
4 tablespoons butter

2 tablespoons olive oil
¾ cup chopped walnuts
6 Belgian endive, stemmed, leaves cut into
   julienne strips lengthwise
12 snow pea pods, stemmed, stringed, blanched
   in boiling water for 1 minute, drained, and
   cut into julienne strips lengthwise

Walnut Oil Dressing:

2 tablespoons white wine vinegar
1 teaspoon Dijon mustard
½ cup walnut oil
Salt and freshly ground pepper to taste

Season each piece of chicken lightly with salt and pepper.

Heat 2 tablespoons of the butter with the oil in a large frying pan and cook the chicken breasts, a few pieces at a time, for about 3 minutes per side over medium-high heat until golden brown. Add a little more oil and butter in equal amounts if necessary.

Cool the chicken.

Meanwhile, make the dressing: Whisk together the vinegar and mustard in a large bowl, drop by drop whisk in the walnut oil, and season to taste with salt and pepper.

Slice the chicken into ¼-inch-thick strips, add to the bowl with the dressing, and turn to coat evenly.

Heat the remaining 2 tablespoons of butter in a large frying pan and cook the walnuts for about 4 minutes, stirring, until toasted. Drain the walnuts, add to the chicken, and toss.

Combine the endive and snow pea pods, line each of four dinner plates with the combination, and spoon equal portions of the chicken and walnuts over the top. Serve immediately.

Serves 4

Cobb Salad

Cobb Salad originated in Hollywood's Brown Derby restaurant in the late thirties. It's certainly California in style, combining fresh-cooked tender bits of chicken breast, avocado, tomatoes, hard-boiled eggs, crunchy bacon, chives, scallions, and Roquefort cheese, tossed with greens and bathed in a heady vinaigrette. It might have been created by one of the current great culinary talents of California cooking, for it is truly a salad of today.

Crusty French or Italian bread, sweet butter, and white wine are all that need be added for a delightful meal.

1 bunch watercress, stemmed, washed, well-
   dried, and chilled

1 small head chicory, washed, well-dried, and
chilled
1 small head romaine, washed, well-dried, and
chilled
2 whole cooked chicken breasts (page 127),
skinned, boned, and cut into ½-inch cubes
3 hard-boiled eggs, diced
2 medium-sized tomatoes, peeled, seeded, and
cubed
1 large firm ripe avocado, peeled, pitted, and
cubed
2 scallions, thinly sliced
2 tablespoons finely chopped fresh chives
8 crisp fried bacon strips, crumbled
2 ounces Roquefort cheese, crumbled

Cobb Salad Vinaigrette:

1½ teaspoons Dijon mustard
⅓ cup white wine vinegar
1 teaspoon Worcestershire sauce
1 teaspoon Cognac
¼ teaspoon salt
Freshly ground pepper to taste
1 cup virgin olive oil

Tear the watercress and chicory into bite-
sized pieces and cut the romaine into ¼-
inch-thick shreds. Toss together and refrigerate until ready to use.

Prepare the dressing: In a small bowl
whisk together the mustard, vinegar, Worcestershire sauce, Cognac, salt, and pepper,
then drop by drop whisk in the oil. Set
aside.

Line a salad bowl with the greens and top
them with the remaining ingredients in the
order that they are given in the recipe.
Whisk the dressing again, pour it over the
salad, and toss it well.

Serve immediately.
Serves 4

Polynesian Chicken and Fruit Salad with Bananas

When a tropical mood strikes, this
sumptuous chicken salad filled with
fruit and garnished with sautéed cashew
nuts and bubbling brown bananas will help
bring the Bali shore closer to home. Serve
with zucchini or carrot bread or any tea
cake, such as lemon cake.

Although I rarely like to garnish food
with inedible flowers, this lovely salad is
one of the exceptions. At our home in St.
Thomas, I garnish it with red, white, and
orange bougainvillaea, and in Long Island I
use white, pink, and purple cosmos.

2 tablespoons butter
⅔ cup raw cashew nuts
3½ cups bite-sized pieces skinned and boned
    cooked chicken (page 127)
1 Delicious apple, cubed
1 cup cubed pineapple
1 cup cubed mango
½ cup shredded coconut
4 hearts of palm, cut into ¼-inch slices
¼ cup thinly sliced scallion
Salt and freshly ground pepper to taste
1 tablespoon melted butter
3 tablespoons dark brown sugar
2 medium-sized bananas, peeled and cut in half
    lengthwise
2 cups shredded Chinese lettuce

Orange-Coconut Dressing:

1 cup mayonnaise or Classic Mayonnaise
    (page 128)
2 tablespoons orange juice
1 tablespoon grenadine
3 tablespoons canned cream of coconut

Heat the butter in a frying pan and cook the cashews until golden brown, stirring often. Remove, pat dry, and cool.

Gently combine the chicken with the ingredients through the scallions in a large bowl.

Mix together the dressing ingredients, turn over the salad, and combine well. Season to taste with salt and pepper.

Toss the melted butter with the brown sugar. Sprinkle equal amounts of the mixture over the bananas, and pass the bananas under the broiler until golden brown.

Spoon the salad onto a large serving platter and surround with the lettuce. Sprinkle the salad with the cashew nuts and garnish with the broiled bananas.

Serves 4

Chicken and Celeriac Salad

When first encountered, celeriac, or celery root, appears most unattractive. What lies inside the knobby, stringy outer covering, though, is an extremely delicately flavored vegetable. Serve this salad with fresh cooked asparagus, sourdough or French bread, sweet butter, and a dry white wine.

2 stalks celery, sliced
2 carrots, peeled and sliced
1 medium-sized onion, coarsely chopped
6 sprigs parsley

1 garlic clove, chopped
3 large chicken breasts, halved
1 whole celeriac (about ¾ pound)
1 quart water
Salt
1 tablespoon lemon juice
12 sprigs watercress, washed and dried

Multi-Herb Vinaigrette:

2 tablespoons Dijon mustard
1 egg yolk, at room temperature
4 tablespoons white wine vinegar or to taste
½ cup virgin olive oil
¼ cup vegetable oil
½ teaspoon dried tarragon
½ teaspoon dried basil
½ teaspoon dried dill
3 tablespoons minced fresh chives
2 tablespoons chopped fresh parsley
2 shallots, minced
Salt and freshly ground pepper to taste

Put the celery, carrots, onion, parsley, and garlic into a 3½-quart saucepan, cover with 1 inch of water, and bring to a boil. Add the chicken and simmer for 20 minutes.

Meanwhile, peel the celeriac and cut it into ¼-inch-thick slices. Cut the slices into matchsticks that are about 1 inch long.

Lightly salt the water and bring it to a boil with the lemon juice. Add the celeriac and simmer for 5 minutes. Drain immediately and refresh under cold running water. Drain and set aside.

Make the dressing: Whisk the mustard, egg yolk, and vinegar together in a medium-sized bowl. Drop by drop whisk in the oils. Stir in the herbs and shallots and season well to taste with salt and pepper. Add the celeriac to the dressing and combine.

Remove the chicken from the liquid in the pan, place in a colander, and run cool tap water over it briefly. When the chicken is cool enough to handle, skin and bone it, and cut it into bite-sized pieces.

Put the chicken into a large bowl. Add the celeriac and dressing and gently toss. Garnish with the watercress sprigs and serve immediately.

Serves 4

Chicken and Sugar Snap Pea Salad

*H*ere is an incredibly easy salad that is made special by caviar-infused mayonnaise. It's a marvelous and quick company dish for summer. (Substitute snow pea pods when sugar snap peas are not in season.) Just double the ingredients to serve eight. Garnish with toast points and tomato wedges.

3½ *cups bite-sized pieces skinned and boned cooked chicken breast (page 127)*
½ *pound sugar snap peas, strings and stem ends removed*
Salt

Caviar-Chive Mayonnaise:
1 *cup chilled mayonnaise or Classic Mayonnaise (page 128)*
¼ *cup red lumpfish caviar*
2 *tablespoons freshly snipped chives*
1 *tablespoon freshly squeezed lemon juice*
Salt and freshly ground pepper to taste

Cook the sugar snap peas in 3 cups of lightly salted boiling water in a saucepan for 3 minutes and drain well.

Put the chicken and sugar snap peas into a bowl and combine.

To make the dressing, blend together the mayonnaise, caviar, chives, and lemon juice in a small bowl and season to taste with salt and pepper.

Turn the dressing over the chicken and combine well. Serve immediately, or cover and refrigerate to serve cold.

Serves 4

Barbecued Chicken and Baked Bean Salad on Toasted Corn Muffins

*S*ometimes we like a certain dish that can claim no culinary greatness whatsoever except that it tastes wonderful and that the repeated requests for it, please, carry a lot of weight. Here is such a salad, made with shredded, freshly barbecued chicken and commercial oven-baked beans, crunchy celery and onions, and served over crisp shredded lettuce on toasted corn muffins. (I use the flat round toaster muffins that are available frozen; they are quite good and the shape is important.) It's an easy, warm meal-in-one salad for the fall and winter seasons; a simple at-home winner.

- 4 large chicken breasts, skinned, boned, and halved
- 1½ cups barbecue sauce (any good or favorite brand)
- 2 cups jarred or canned oven-baked beans (do not use pork and beans)
- ½ cup diced celery
- ¼ cup chopped red onion
- 1 teaspoon mustard
- 4 toaster corn muffins
- 1½ cups finely shredded iceberg lettuce
- 12 celery sticks
- 12 carrot sticks

Marinate the chicken breast halves, covered, in 1 cup of the barbecue sauce in the refrigerator for 1 hour.

Barbecue the chicken until done; then cool.

Meanwhile, heat the beans.

When the chicken is cool enough to handle, tear it into shreds and put it into a large bowl with the celery, onion, and beans.

Combine the remaining ½ cup of barbecue sauce and the mustard in a small saucepan and bring to a boil. Immediately remove from the heat, add to the chicken mixture, and combine.

Toast the muffins and put one on each of four dinner plates. Arrange equal amounts of the lettuce over the muffins and spoon the salad over the top.

Garnish each dish with three celery sticks and three carrot sticks and serve immediately.

Serves 4

Grilled Chicken Breast and Sun-Dried Tomato Salad

This mouth-watering dish is great for a quick summer meal. Serve with corn on the cob and complete the meal with strawberry shortcake.

- 4 large chicken breasts, boned, skinned, and halved
- Olive oil
- Salt and freshly ground pepper to taste
- 1 large bunch watercress, washed, dried, and stemmed
- 1 small head chicory (curly endive), washed, dried, and torn into bite-sized pieces
- 12 sun-dried tomatoes, cut into thin strips

Dressing:

1 tablespoon sherry wine vinegar
1 tablespoon red wine vinegar
1 tablespoon freshly squeezed lemon juice
½ cup virgin olive oil
½ teaspoon dried basil
Salt and freshly ground pepper to taste

Brush the chicken breast halves lightly with oil and season lightly with salt and pepper.

Heat a barbecue grill or ridged iron frying pan and spray with nonstick vegetable oil. Cook the chicken on each side for about 4 minutes, or just until done, a few pieces at a time. (If you don't have a grill or ridged frying pan, cook on a rack under a hot broiler.)

Transfer the cooked chicken to a cutting board and cut each breast half lengthwise into four strips.

Arrange the watercress and chicory in equal amounts on four dinner plates. Top with equal portions of the chicken and sun-dried tomatoes.

Make the dressing: Whisk together the vinegars and lemon juice, drop by drop whisk in the oil, add the basil, and season to taste with salt and pepper.

Spoon the dressing equally over the salads. Serve immediately.

Serves 4

Chicken and Cucumber Salad with Dill

Chicken and Cucumber Salad with Dill is another superb and easy main course salad for any season. The dish can be transformed into a curried chicken salad by replacing the dill with 1 tablespoon of curry powder and adding ½ teaspoon of ground turmeric. Serve the curried salad with mango chutney, if desired. Accompany either version with toasted pita bread.

4 large cooked chicken breasts (page 127), skinned, boned, and cut into ½-inch cubes
2 medium-sized cucumbers, peeled and cut in half lengthwise
8 whole leaves red radicchio

Dilled Dressing:

½ cup mayonnaise or Classic Mayonnaise (page 128)
¼ cup sour cream
1 tablespoon freshly squeezed lemon juice
1 tablespoon chopped fresh dill, or 1 teaspoon dried dill
Salt and freshly ground pepper to taste

4 scallions, all the white and 1 inch of the green thinly sliced

Put the chicken into a large bowl.

With a teaspoon, scrape the seeds out of the center of each cucumber half and discard. Cut the cucumbers into ½-inch cubes and add to the chicken.

Then make the dressing: In a medium-sized bowl combine the mayonnaise, sour cream, lemon juice, and dill, and season with salt and pepper to taste. Stir all but 1 rounded tablespoon of the scallions into the mixture.

Add the dressing to the chicken and cucumbers and combine well. Add a little more mayonnaise if a creamier consistency is desired.

Spoon equal amounts of the salad onto the center of each of four dinner plates. Tuck the stem ends of two radicchio leaves ½ inch under each salad on opposite sides and sprinkle the tops of the salads equally with the remaining scallions. Serve immediately, or cover and chill to serve cold.

NOTE: A tablespoon of finely chopped fresh mint, or 1 teaspoon of dried mint, added to the dressing makes a delicious and unusual variation.

Serves 4

Peking Chicken Salad in Lettuce Cups

The recipe for this incredibly delicious chicken salad originally came from Mary Eustis of Massachusetts as an appetizer. It is still an easy, first-rate hors d'oeuvre. Here, however, the succulent meat is removed from the chicken wing bones and is wrapped, along with the sauce, in lettuce leaves with a piece of scallion to make a fabulous hand-held salad reminiscent of Peking duck, but considerably easier to prepare. The salad can also be served in a more traditional manner, mounded in the center of individual dinner plates surrounded with shredded lettuce and garnished with the scallions. Steamed seasonal vegetables like zucchini and yellow squash or canned or jarred miniature corn cobs, seasoned lightly with Oriental sesame oil, make a fine accompaniment.

36 chicken wings
1 cup soy sauce
½ cup granulated sugar
1 cup packed dark brown sugar
24 large whole iceberg lettuce leaves
12 scallions, white parts only, cut in half lengthwise

Preheat the oven to 325°.

Cut off the wing tips and freeze them for making stock. Cut each of the wings into two pieces at the joint and divide the pieces into two shallow roasting pans.

In a bowl combine the soy sauce and sugars and pour the mixture over the chicken in each pan in equal amounts. Turn the parts to coat them evenly.

Bake on the middle shelf of the oven for 30 minutes. (If both pans won't fit on one shelf, put one on the lower shelf and one on the middle shelf.)

Remove both pans, turn the pieces of chicken with tongs, and return the pans to the oven for 30 minutes. (If using two shelves, reverse the order, so that the one that was on the bottom shelf is now on the middle shelf, and vice versa.)

Turn the wings again and cook for about 20 minutes (reversing the shelf order again), or until the wings are rich and dark brown in color with the meat nearly falling off the bones, but take care not to burn them.

Allow the chicken to cool until you can handle it comfortably. With the aid of a small sharp knife, remove the meat and skins in shreds and place into a large bowl, along with any sauce left in the pans.

Spoon the mixture into the center of the lettuce leaves in equal portions, top each with half a scallion, and roll up. Serve at room temperature. Make in advance and serve cold, if desired.

Serves 6

Lemon Chicken and Cilantro Salad

Cilantro (also known as coriander) has an assertive flavor which is quite unique and impossible to describe if you haven't tried it. I think of it as a peppery, grassy-fresh flavor. Generally you either like it very much or not at all. It is widely used in East Indian, Chinese, and Mexican cooking. Here, a fragrant Mexican sauce tops tender chicken breasts, and marination allows the flavors of the piquant dressing to further develop. Accompany with steamed carrot slices and crusty French or Italian bread to soak up the delicious sauce.

4 cooked chicken breasts (page 127), skinned, boned, and thinly sliced

Cilantro Sauce:
2 tablespoons freshly squeezed lemon juice
2 tablespoons red wine vinegar
½ cup virgin olive oil

¼ cup dry red wine
1 tablespoon Worcestershire sauce
1½ tablespoons Bovril
1 clove garlic, minced
½ cup minced onion
1 large red bell pepper, cored, seeded, and diced
½ cup chopped fresh cilantro
½ cup chopped fresh parsley
Salt and freshly ground pepper to taste

Arrange the chicken slices in a shallow dish with at least 1-inch-high sides.

Combine the sauce ingredients in a heavy saucepan and simmer for 10 minutes. Cool.

Spoon the sauce over the chicken, cover, and refrigerate for 2 hours before serving. **Serves 4**

Curried Turkey and Wild Rice Salad

I originally created this elegant salad to use up leftover turkey and wild rice from a Thanksgiving dinner. It has now become our traditional meal the day after that holiday, along with cranberry sauce, French bread, and honey butter.* Cooked chicken, duck, or ham can be substituted for the turkey in the recipe.

2½ cups cubed cooked turkey
2½ cups cooked wild rice (1 cup uncooked rice)
½ cup unsweetened coconut flakes
½ cup toasted almond slivers (page 47)
¾ cup thinly sliced celery
½ cup dark raisins
1 medium green bell pepper, cored, seeded, and diced
2 scallions, thinly sliced
1 cup canned pineapple chunks, drained
1 cup seedless green grapes
2 tablespoons fresh-grated orange zest
8 leaves romaine lettuce, washed and dried (optional)

Curried Orange-Lime Mayonnaise:

1½ cups mayonnaise or Classic Mayonnaise (page 128)
2 tablespoons orange juice
1 tablespoon fresh lime juice (reduce a bit if using Classic Mayonnaise)
2 tablespoons curry powder
Salt and freshly ground pepper to taste

Gently toss all the salad ingredients except the lettuce together in a large bowl.

Mix together the dressing ingredients in a medium bowl and pour over the salad.

Combine the mixture well. Serve immediately, or cover, and thoroughly chill. Serve cold on romaine lettuce leaves, if desired.
Serves 4

* To make honey butter: Whisk together 3 tablespoons of honey with a stick of softened butter, and chill in a small bowl until served.

Smoked Turkey, Mozzarella, and Tomato Salad with Fried Capers

Mozzarella and fresh ripe tomato slices with fresh basil, drizzled with fruity olive oil and sprinkled with freshly ground pepper, is a simple but magnificent salad or appetizer that has become very popular. I like the combination so much that I've extended the dish and developed a main course salad by adding smoked turkey breast on a blanket of arugula, topped with a basil and red onion relish and fried capers.

Serve with sesame-seed-topped crusty Italian bread and sweet butter.

1 large bunch arugula, washed, dried, and stem ends trimmed
1 pound mozzarella, thinly sliced
2 large ripe tomatoes, thinly sliced
1 pound thinly sliced smoked turkey breast
Fruity extra-virgin olive oil
Freshly ground pepper to taste

Basil and Red Onion Relish:

¼ cup finely chopped fresh basil (do not substitute dried basil)
½ cup diced red onion

Fried Capers:

2 cups peanut oil
⅓ cup large capers, drained and patted dry

Line a large serving platter with the arugula. Arrange alternating slices of mozzarella, tomato slices, and smoked turkey over it.

Make the relish by combining the basil and red onion in a small bowl; set aside.

Then fry the capers: Heat the peanut oil and cook the capers until they open up and are crisp, stirring often. Drain.

Drizzle olive oil lightly over the salad. Spoon the relish over the top, sprinkle with freshly ground pepper and the capers, and serve.
Serves 4

Turkey Hash Salad with Sour Cream Dressing

*T*he vital ingredient for any hash dish is sautéed onions; they give this salad its hearty aromatic flavor. Turkey Hash Salad is a natural for picnics, tailgates, or half-time in-front-of-the-TV dinners.

Serve with a side salad of mixed greens tossed in basic vinaigrette (page 18).

3 *cups cooked turkey, cut into bite-sized pieces*
1 *pound small new potatoes, boiled, cooled, peeled and cut into bite-sized pieces*
1 *large green bell pepper, cored, seeded, and diced*
3 *tablespoons butter*
3 *tablespoons vegetable oil*
1 *cup coarsely chopped onion*
1 *teaspoon Worcestershire sauce*

Sour Cream Dressing II:

½ *cup sour cream*
½ *cup mayonnaise or Classic Mayonnaise (page 128)*
2 *tablespoons Dijon mustard*
2 *tablespoons chopped fresh parsley*
Salt and freshly ground pepper to taste

Put the turkey, new potatoes, and green pepper in a large bowl.

Heat the butter and oil in a large frying pan and cook the onions for about 10 minutes over medium-high heat, stirring often, until golden but not burned. Drain and cool in a colander.

Combine the dressing ingredients in a small bowl and season well to taste with salt and pepper.

Put the onions in a small bowl, add the Worcestershire sauce, and stir, and let rest a moment or two.

Meanwhile, turn the dressing over the turkey mixture and combine well. Add the onions and blend them into the mixture. Serve immediately.

Serves 4

Turkey Salad Veronique in a Bread Bowl

When applied to food, the name Veronique usually means that grapes are included in the dish. Seedless green grapes plus pitted cherries are folded into this marvelously moist turkey salad, and when available, succulent tiny California purple champagne grapes, found at certain times of the year in quality produce markets.

For a spectacular presentation, a round loaf of country French bread, called a boule, is hollowed out and serves as the salad bowl. As the salad is eaten, cut wedges out of the edible bowl and serve. This is a takeoff on medieval dining, when a large slice of bread was the diner's plate. Serve with lemonade.

3½ cups cooked dark and light meat turkey, cut into bite-sized pieces
1 cup seedless green grapes
½ cup tiny purple champagne grapes (optional)
1 cup pitted fresh cherries
½ cup diced celery
½ cup pecan halves
1 10-inch-round loaf crusty French bread

1 tablespoon chopped fresh parsley
Parsley sprigs

Orange Mayonnaise:

1¼ cups mayonnaise or Classic Mayonnaise (page 128)
½ cup sour cream
1 teaspoon sugar
2 tablespoons orange juice
Salt and freshly ground pepper to taste

Combine the turkey, grapes, cherries, celery, and pecans in a large bowl.

To make the dressing, mix together the mayonnaise, sour cream, sugar, and orange juice in a small bowl, and add salt and pepper to taste.

Turn the dressing over the salad and mix well.

Slice about 1 inch off the top of the loaf of bread, in one piece, and reserve to use as a top. Carefully hollow out most of the bread inside the loaf with your fingers and save for another use, such as bread crumbs, leaving the crust and ½ inch of the white part of the bread intact.

Make a small incision in the center of the top of the bread lid and stick the parsley sprigs into it.

Spoon the salad into the bread bowl, place the stuffed bread bowl on a serving platter, and tilt the garnished bread lid

against the side. Sprinkle the top of the salad with the chopped parsley and serve.
Serves 4

Turkey and Cherry Tomato Salad with Mustard-Dill Dressing

Coated with pungent sweetened mustard-dill dressing, this salad is another delicious way to use leftover turkey. If desired, serve as an opened-faced sandwich on toasted bagels or rye bread.

3½ cups chopped cooked light and dark meat turkey
1 cup halved cherry tomatoes

Mustard-Dill Dressing:

½ cup Dijon mustard
4 tablespoons sugar
¼ cup red wine vinegar
¼ cup olive oil
⅓ cup vegetable oil
2 tablespoons chopped fresh dill, or
    1 tablespoon dried dill
Freshly ground pepper to taste

Combine the turkey and cherry tomatoes in a large bowl.

Mix together the dressing ingredients in a small jar, turn over the salad, and combine well.

Serve immediately, or cover and chill thoroughly. Serve cold and retoss.
Serves 4

Cornish Game Hen and Vegetable Salad

Cornish game hens cut into individual serving pieces and gently pan-fried in butter are extraordinarily succulent and tender. Fried Cornish pieces are the centerpiece of this wonderful meal-in-one-dish salad, which also includes baby zucchini, corn, and French green beans on Boston lettuce leaves, and a heady hazelnut oil dressing.

4 Cornish game hens, cut into 6 pieces each in same manner as cut-up chicken (2 legs, 2 thighs, and 1 halved breast—discard wings or save for another use)
Garlic powder
Salt and freshly ground pepper

145

Flour
2 sticks butter (8 ounces)
4 tablespoons vegetable oil
2 cups water
Salt
1½ cups unpeeled baby zucchini, cut into
   ¼-inch-thick slices
1 10-ounce package frozen corn kernels,
   thawed and drained
½ pound fresh French green beans, stems
   trimmed
8 large Boston lettuce leaves, washed and dried

Hazelnut Oil Dressing I:

¼ cup white wine vinegar
2 tablespoons finely chopped shallot
1 tablespoon Dijon mustard
½ cup hazelnut oil

Lightly season each Cornish game hen piece with garlic powder, salt, and pepper. Coat each piece lightly with flour.

The meat will have to be cooked in two batches as follows. Heat 1 stick of the butter and 2 tablespoons of the oil in a large frying pan and add half of the seasoned and flour-coated Cornish pieces. Cook over medium heat for 10 minutes and turn the pieces with tongs. Lower the heat slightly and cook about 10 minutes longer or until golden brown and tender. Drain. Clean the pan, heat the remaining stick of butter and 2 tablespoons of oil and cook the remaining Cornish pieces in the same manner. (If you have two large frying pans, cook both batches at the same time.)

Meanwhile, make the dressing: Put the vinegar and shallots into a small, heavy-bottomed saucepan and reduce the vinegar to 1 tablespoon over high heat, stirring often. Immediately remove the pan from the heat and whisk in the mustard and the hazelnut oil. Set aside.

Lightly salt the water, bring it to a boil in a 2½-quart saucepan, and cook the vegetables for exactly 4 minutes, stirring occasionally. Drain, refresh them under cold water, and drain well.

Line each of four large dinner plates with two Boston lettuce leaves. Put six Cornish pieces in the center of each plate and surround with equal amounts of the vegetables. Spoon the dressing over the salads equally. Serve immediately.

Serves 4

Warm Duck and Sauerkraut Salad with Raspberry Vinegar

An elegant fall and winter main course salad, the duck, sauerkraut, raspberry vinegar, and crisp skin cracklings combination produces a magnificent marriage of contrasting flavors and textures. Serve with fresh salad greens, French bread, and dry red wine.

1 whole boned large duck breast,* separated lengthwise
Salt and freshly ground pepper
2 tablespoons olive oil
4 tablespoons sweet butter
½ cup diced peeled Delicious apple
½ cup canned or homemade chicken broth or stock
1 cup rinsed and well-drained canned sauerkraut
3 tablespoons raspberry vinegar

Season the duck all over with salt and pepper. Heat the oil and 2 tablespoons of the butter in a medium frying pan and cook the duck, skin side down, for 5 minutes. Turn and cook for 5 more minutes. Remove the duck from the pan and remove the pan from the heat.

With the help of a fork and a small sharp knife and/or kitchen scissors, remove the skin from each piece of duck by cutting between the meat and the fat under the skin. Cut the skin into small pieces.

Return the pan to the heat and add the duck, removed-skin side down, and the duck skin pieces. Cook for 3 minutes, then remove the duck. Increase the heat, and stir and turn the skins until crisp. Remove and drain on paper towels.

Pour out all of the fat in the pan and add the remaining 2 tablespoons of butter. When the butter has melted, add the apples and cook for 2 minutes over medium heat. Turn the heat to high and add the chicken stock, sauerkraut, and vinegar. Stirring constantly, cook for 3 minutes. Remove from the heat.

Carve the duck into thin slices and arrange a layered row of duck down the center of two dinner plates. Spoon the sauerkraut mixture equally over the top and sprinkle each with the cracklings. Serve immediately.

Serves 2

* Fresh or frozen boned duck breasts are available at fine butchers and specialty food shops.

Duck, Gruyère, and Endive Salad with Cantaloupe

Duck lends itself readily to the new styles of salad preparation. Here's an offering that's particularly appealing in the spring or summer. The combination is set off by a zesty green peppercorn dressing. Simply serve with French bread and sweet butter.

2½ cups shredded cooked duck meat (page 127)
1½ cups grated Gruyère cheese
1½ cups thinly sliced Belgian endive, leaves separated
1 small cantaloupe, peeled, seeded, and thinly sliced

Green Peppercorn Dressing:

1 tablespoon minced shallot
3 tablespoons red wine vinegar
1 teaspoon Dijon mustard
1 teaspoon drained green peppercorns
¼ cup hazelnut oil
¼ cup olive oil
Salt and freshly ground pepper to taste

Combine the duck, cheese, and endive in a large bowl.

Make the dressing: Whisk together the shallots, vinegar, mustard, and green peppercorns; drop by drop whisk in the oils; then season to taste with salt and pepper.

Pour the dressing over the salad and toss well.

Divide the salad among four dinner plates and arrange equal portions of cantaloupe slices in a circle around each salad. Serve immediately.

Serves 4

Waldorf Salad with Duck and Red Currant Sauce

The dates, walnut oil, and duck used here elevate a basic salad right into the ranks of a salad of today. Serve with black bread or French Walnut Bread (page 32) and sweet butter.

1¼ cups diced Delicious apple
1¼ cups seedless green grapes
12 pitted dates, chopped
⅔ cup finely diced celery
⅔ cup chopped walnuts

2 tablespoons sweet butter
1 tablespoon vegetable oil
2 whole large magret or Long Island duck
   breasts, halved, skinned, and boned
Salt and freshly ground pepper to taste
½ cup red currant jelly
1 tablespoon water
8 sprigs watercress, washed and dried

Waldorf Dressing:

⅔ cup mayonnaise or Classic Mayonnaise
   (page 128)
1 tablespoon walnut oil
2 teaspoons freshly squeezed lemon juice
1 teaspoon sugar
¼ teaspoon ground ginger

Combine the apple, grapes, dates, celery, and walnuts in a large bowl.

In another bowl make the dressing: Whisk together the mayonnaise, walnut oil, lemon juice, sugar, and ginger.

Turn the mixture over the salad and lightly toss. Cover and refrigerate until serving.

Just before serving the salad, heat the butter with the oil in a large frying pan. Cook the duck breasts over medium heat for about 4 minutes per side for medium-rare, a minute or two longer per side for medium. Season the breasts with salt and pepper to taste, and let rest for 5 minutes.

Meanwhile, heat the red currant jelly in a small saucepan with the water, and whisk constantly until liquefied.

Spoon equal amounts of the Waldorf Salad over one side of each of four dinner plates.

Thinly slice each duck breast half on the diagonal and arrange on the other side of the plates. Spoon equal amounts of the currant sauce over the duck breasts, and garnish the plates with two watercress sprigs each. Serve immediately.

Serves 4

HAM AND SAUSAGE SALADS

Ham and sausage main course salads always create an element of surprise when served. Perhaps that is because they are not ordinarily thought of when planning a menu based on a salad. However, the addictive robust flavor of the different kinds of sausages—hot, sweet, or spicy—and the honest, full flavor of various hams, smoked or unsmoked, enable these versatile foods to be serious contenders for creative main course salads. All kinds of dressings can be used successfully, too. I predict that we'll be seeing a lot more ham and sausage main course salads on restaurant menus everywhere.

The ham and sausage salads making up this chapter are just a few of the possible seductive salads in this growing category. They range from the reintroduction of soothing old-fashioned ham salad to the arresting, pungent Grilled Sausage, Arugula, and Marinated Red Pepper Salad.

In addition, the recipe for a beautiful elegant salad of fruit wrapped in prosciutto can be found in the fruit chapter.

After developing this recipe, I tested a mixed green and vegetable salad, tossed in a balsamic vinaigrette dressing, prepared with prosciutto enveloping the combined ingredients in the same manner. It was excellent, and the recipe is included in the vegetable chapter.

ECIPES

Old-Fashioned Ham Salad
Black Forest Ham and Brie Salad
Ratatouille and Sausage Salad
Grilled Sausage, Arugula, and Marinated Red Pepper Salad
Kielbasa and Corn Salad
Sweet Potato Salad with Baked Ham

Old-Fashioned Ham Salad

When I was a child in Kansas, ham salad sandwiches were more popular than tunafish. The reverse is true today, of course. Ham salad has not been maligned so much as it's been forgotten. I still crave the uncomplicated plain ham salad of yesterday. Freshly made, accented with crisp greens and ripe tomatoes and served with toasted garlic bread, ham salad is a comfort food worth remembering.

2½ cups diced boiled ham
¾ cup diced celery
3 tablespoons diced gherkin pickle
¾ cup mayonnaise or Classic Mayonnaise (page 128)
2 tablespoons chili sauce
3 cups mixed watercress and Boston lettuce, washed, dried and torn into bite-sized pieces
4 small tomatoes, stem ends cut off, each cut into 4 wedges
1 recipe Garlic Bread

In a large bowl combine the ham, celery, pickle, mayonnaise, and chili sauce. Cover the salad, refrigerate and chill for several hours.

Combine the greens and arrange on each of four dinner plates. Spoon equal portions of the ham salad on each plate, garnish each with four tomato wedges, and serve with the garlic bread.
Serves 4

Toasted Garlic Bread

4 tablespoons softened butter
1 garlic clove, finely chopped
8 1-inch-thick slices Italian or French bread

Just before serving the salad, combine the butter and garlic and spread evenly over the side of each of the bread slices. Toast the bread, buttered side up, under the broiler until golden.
Makes 8 slices

Black Forest Ham and Brie Salad

Salad-topping, Brie-covered pumpernickel slices bring a slightly different and enjoyable dimension to salad-making. Very little dressing is used to mix the actual salad, for it shouldn't overwhelm the Brie. Olive oil can be put on the table for those who like a moister salad.

Sometimes I include one small diced avocado and eight crumbled crisp-cooked bacon strips in the salad mixture, too, for variety.

8 slices pumpernickel bread
10 ounces ripe Brie, at room temperature
1 small bunch watercress, washed, dried, and stemmed
12 leaves of heart of romaine lettuce, washed, dried, and torn into bite-sized pieces
½ cup diced radish
¾ pound Black Forest ham, thinly sliced, cut crosswise into ¼-inch strips
16 cornichon pickles

Dressing:

1 tablespoon white wine vinegar
⅓ cup fruity extra-virgin olive oil
Salt and freshly ground pepper to taste

Spread one side of each slice of bread with equal amounts of the cheese. Put two cheese-covered slices of the bread on each of four dinner plates.

In a bowl combine the watercress, romaine, radish, and ham.

Whisk together the vinegar and oil in a small bowl, and season to taste with salt and pepper. Pour the dressing over the salad and toss well.

Spoon equal amounts of the salad over the bread slices, garnish with the pickles, and serve.

Serves 4

Ratatouille and Sausage Salad

Ratatouille, the wonderful vegetable ragout from Provence, makes a delicious cold salad accented with warm sausage. Because this ratatouille is served as a salad, the cooking time is shorter than for the standard ratatouille so that the vegetables won't be too soft. The salad can be accompanied by French bread and butter, of course, but for a change, I toast bagel halves and pass butter or creamy mascarpone.*

4 sweet Italian sausages
½ cup virgin olive oil
1 medium-large onion, chopped
1 teaspoon minced garlic
2 green bell peppers, cored, seeded, and cut lengthwise into ¼-inch-thick strips
3 cups unpeeled eggplant, cut into ¾-inch cubes

2 medium-sized zucchini, cut into ½-inch
   cubes
2 cups seeded and diced tomato
1 tablespoon chopped fresh basil, or
   1 teaspoon dried basil
½ teaspoon dried oregano
¼ teaspoon dried thyme
Pinch of dried rosemary
3 tablespoons dry white wine
Salt and freshly ground pepper to taste

Prick each sausage in several places with the point of a sharp knife. Bring 1 inch of water to a boil in a saucepan and simmer the sausages for 15 minutes.

Meanwhile, heat ¼ cup of the olive oil in a heavy 4-quart pot. Add the onion, garlic, and peppers and cook over medium heat for 3 minutes, stirring often.

Add the eggplant, zucchini, tomatoes, herbs, and wine, and combine. Season to taste with salt and pepper. Simmer, covered, for 15 minutes. Stir and simmer 15 minutes more, uncovered.

Drain and cool the sausages. When cool, cover and refrigerate.

When the ratatouille is cooked, taste for seasoning and transfer to a bowl to cool. When cool, cover and refrigerate for several hours.

About 20 minutes before serving the salad, cut the sausages into ¼-inch-thick slices. Heat the remaining ¼ cup of olive oil in a frying pan and cook the sausage slices until golden brown. Drain.

With a large slotted spoon, put equal amounts of the ratatouille on four dinner plates and surround with equal portions of the sausage slices.

Serves 4

* Mascarpone, found in the cheese department of specialty food stores, especially Italian, is actually a condensed or solidified cream. Hand-whipped softened cream cheese can replace the mascarpone.

Grilled Sausage, Arugula, and Marinated Red Pepper Salad

*T*he combined assertive flavors in this salad are wonderful, but the best part is that it's so simple and quick to prepare. Serve with Italian bread and sweet butter. The salad also makes great hero sandwiches on Italian bread.

> 2 *large red bell peppers, cored, seeded, and quartered lengthwise*
> 4 *sweet Italian sausages*
> 4 *hot Italian sausages*
> 1 *large bunch arugula, washed, dried, and stem ends trimmed*

Anchovy Dressing II:

¼ *cup red wine vinegar*
1 *tablespoon drained and mashed anchovy fillets*
1 *tablespoon minced shallot*
½ *cup olive oil*
Salt and freshly ground pepper to taste

Peel the skins of the pepper quarters with the aid of a vegetable peeler and cut the skinned pepper into thin strips. Put the pepper strips into a bowl.

To make the dressing, combine the vinegar, anchovies, shallots, and olive oil in a small bowl and season with salt and pepper.

Pour the dressing over the pepper strips and let rest at room temperature for 30 minutes, turning once.

Grill the sausages until golden brown on an outdoor grill or on a ridged skillet, about 20 minutes. Cool and cut into ¼-inch slices, lengthwise.

Arrange the arugula on each of four dinner plates and top with the sausages in equal amounts. Spoon the marinated peppers over the sausages in equal portions. Serve immediately.

Serves 4

Kielbasa and Corn Salad

*K*ielbasa is delicious, readily available everywhere, quick to prepare, and relatively inexpensive. A menu featuring this pleasing fall or winter salad might begin with New England clam chowder and end with a carrot spice cake.

3 tablespoons peanut oil

1½ pounds kielbasa sausage, cut into ¼-inch-
thick slices

1 10-ounce package frozen corn, cooked and
drained

½ cup diced cored and seeded green bell pepper

¼ cup thinly sliced scallion

3 cups bite-sized pieces chicory (curly endive),
washed and dried

Sweetened Mustard Dressing:

3 tablespoons red wine vinegar

2 tablespoons brown sugar

2 tablespoons whole-grain mustard

⅔ cup peanut or safflower oil

Salt and freshly ground pepper to taste

Heat the oil in a large frying pan and cook the kielbasa slices over medium heat until golden brown on each side. Drain.

Combine the corn, green pepper, and scallions in a large bowl and add the kielbasa.

To make the dressing, whisk together the vinegar, brown sugar, and mustard until the sugar dissolves; drop by drop whisk in the oil; then season to taste with salt and pepper.

Pour the dressing over the salad and toss.

Line a serving platter with the lettuce and top with the salad. Serve immediately.

Serves 4

Sweet Potato Salad with Baked Ham

An unusual blend of ingredients creates this tempting salad that can be savored any season of the year. It's an adaptation of a dish sampled at Caneel Bay resort in St. John in the United States Virgin Islands. Spoon the salad onto lettuce leaves and serve with French green beans and Pan Corn Bread (page 17).

2 pounds sweet potatoes

4 ounces cream cheese, softened to room
temperature

1 cup mayonnaise or Classic Mayonnaise
(page 128)

1 teaspoon Worcestershire sauce

2 dashes hot sauce, such as Tabasco

½ cup currants

¼ cup thinly sliced scallion

1 tablespoon minced fresh chives

1 cup diced unpeeled Delicious red apple

2 cups baked ham, cut into ¾-inch cubes

Salt and freshly ground pepper

Preheat the oven to 400°.

Bake the potatoes in the oven on a baking sheet or a sheet of foil for about 40 minutes or until tender, turning once, halfway through the cooking time. Cool for 45 minutes.

In a large bowl, whip the cream cheese with a wire whisk until creamy. Add the mayonnaise, Worcestershire, hot sauce, currants, scallions, and chives and mix thoroughly.

Slice the sweet potatoes crosswise into ½-inch pieces, and remove the skins. Cut the sweet potatoes into ½-inch cubes.

Add the potatoes, apples, and ham to the cream cheese mixture and gently fold together. Season to taste with salt and pepper and combine. Serve immediately or cover and chill thoroughly.

Serves 4

LAMB AND PORK SALADS

Lamb and pork main course salads have finally come into their own in America, and are now recognized as excellent foods for main course salads of substance. They offer a distinctive alternative to poultry and beef and, of course, lamb and pork can be substituted for beef or chicken in many recipes.

Cubed leftover cooked pork, sliced scallions, pineapple, and rice in a yogurt dressing with cilantro make a lovely, unexpected last-minute meal.

A grilled butterflied leg of lamb, sliced, cut into strips, and tossed with string beans and a fragrant vinaigrette dressing is an ideal salad for summer entertaining. In the winter, one might substitute lima beans for the string beans and combine in a warm vinaigrette dressing. The recipe follows.

The lamb and pork recipes in this chapter are all delicious, a bit unusual, and quite simple to prepare.

Recipes

Lamb and Raita Salad

Grilled Lamb and Green Bean Salad

Lamb and Olive Salad

Greek Salad with Marinated Lamb Meatballs

Pork Tenderloin and Mushroom Salad

Curried Pork and Peach Salad with Sautéed Cashew Nuts

Pork and Black Bean Chili Salad
with Cheese and Green Chili Quesadillas

Lamb and Raita Salad

Raita is the lovely, refreshing East Indian condiment made of combined cucumber and yogurt. The addition of lamb, green peppers, and scallions to raita results in a wonderfully cooling summer salad. The lamb I use most often in this salad is leftover barbecued butterflied leg of lamb (page 167), which imparts a subtle grilled flavor. Serve the salad on a bed of greens, if desired.

Poppadums are a perfect foil for this salad. East Indian biscuits or crackers that puff up and crisp after being cooked only a few seconds in oil, poppadums are made with lentil and rice flour and have a unique and addictive flavor. Poppadums can be found in specialty food shops, especially East Indian ones. Take care to purchase plain ones, not those labeled "spicy," which are *extremely* spicy and hot. If unavailable, serve toasted pita bread instead.

1 medium cucumber, peeled, halved, seeded, and cubed
Salt
1½ cups plain yogurt
½ teaspoon sugar
3½ cups cubed cooked lamb
1 medium green pepper, cored, seeded, and diced
¼ cup thinly sliced scallion
Salt and freshly ground pepper to taste

Put the cucumber cubes in a colander, sprinkle lightly with salt, and let drain for 30 minutes in the sink or over a plate.

Rinse the cucumber and pat dry.

In a large bowl combine the cucumber with the remaining ingredients through the salt and pepper. Cover and refrigerate for several hours.

Just before serving the salad, make the poppadums and serve hot.

NOTE: Mint is used too often with lamb, perhaps, but if you like the combination as much as I do, ¼ cup of chopped fresh mint can be added to this recipe.

Serves 4

Poppadums

Peanut or vegetable oil
1 4-ounce package imported poppadums

Heat ¼ inch of oil in a large frying pan and cook the poppadums (10 to 12), a few at a time, until crisp and puffy—this requires only a few seconds per side. Drain on paper towels and serve hot.

Makes 10 to 12

Grilled Lamb and Green Bean Salad

This is a wonderful salad for *al fresco* dining in the spring or summer. The marinated grilled lamb featured in this recipe imparts a subtle smoked flavor to this lovely salad. The recipe for the lamb comes from Dr. Bruce McClennan, a professor of radiology at Washington University in St. Louis, Missouri, an old friend who is very particular about his lamb.

Accompany with French bread, halved cherry tomatoes lightly tossed in a combination of mayonnaise, chopped fresh dill, and lemon juice, and, for dessert, a chocolate mousse with raspberries, or, if the meal is served outdoors, double-dip coffee ice cream cones.

Keep in mind when preparing this recipe that the lamb marinates overnight.

6 pound leg of lamb, boned and butterflied*
   (have butcher do this, if desired)
2 pounds green beans, ends trimmed

Marinade:

1 cup dry red wine
3 tablespoons red wine vinegar
2 tablespoons soy sauce
1 teaspoon dried rosemary
1 clove garlic, minced
½ teaspoon salt
Freshly ground pepper to taste

Dressing:

¼ cup red wine vinegar
1 tablespoon Dijon mustard
1 teaspoon minced garlic
1 egg yolk, at room temperature
½ cup virgin olive oil
½ cup vegetable oil
2 tablespoons chopped fresh parsley
Salt and freshly ground pepper to taste

Put the meat in a shallow roasting pan. Mix the marinade ingredients together in a bowl, pour over the meat, cover, and refrigerate overnight, or at least 6 hours, turning occasionally.

To cook, place the meat fat side down on a double thickness of heavy-duty aluminum foil over hot coals. Use a kettle-style or lid-top grill or make a hood for the grill out of foil. Cover and cook for 15 minutes. Turn the lamb and cook for 15 more minutes for a good pink color; cook 5 minutes longer if you want it better done.

Meanwhile, prepare the dressing: Combine the vinegar, mustard, garlic, and egg yolk in a bowl with a wire whisk. Drop by drop whisk in the oil. Add the parsley and season to taste with salt and pepper. Let rest.

Cook the green beans covered with lightly salted slowly boiling water for exactly 4 minutes. Drain immediately and refresh under cold running water. Drain well, put into a large shallow bowl, and let cool.

When the lamb has cooked, let it rest for ten minutes before cutting it into thin slices, against the grain. Cut each slice of meat into strips about ½ inch wide. Add the lamb strips to the bowl with the green beans and turn the dressing over the salad. Toss gently and taste for seasoning.

Serve immediately or chilled. If chilled, bring back to room temperature before serving and retoss.

Serves 8

* Boning and butterflying the lamb is quite simple. Cut along the leg lengthwise through to the bone. Remove the tendons as you go. Peel the meat back, stripping the bone clean. You will be left with a fairly large, flat piece of meat with fat on one side. Trim off excess fat, but leave a ¼-inch layer of fat. The meat should be fairly uniform in thickness and will need to be flattened in some spots. To do this make shallow incisions in the thick parts and lightly pound with a tenderizer mallet.

Lamb and Olive Salad

This savory lamb salad is a great way to use leftover roast leg of lamb. Serve with crusty Italian or French bread slices spread with sweet butter and sprinkled with freshly ground pepper.

2 tablespoons butter
½ cup pine nuts
3 cups cooked lamb, cut into bite-sized pieces
¾ cup chopped black Greek olives
Salt and freshly ground pepper to taste
1 quart spinach, washed, dried, and torn into bite-sized pieces
1 tablespoon chopped fresh parsley

Lemon-Mint Dressing:

1 cup mayonnaise or Classic Mayonnaise (page 128)
1 tablespoon whole grain mustard
1 small garlic clove, minced
1 tablespoon freshly squeezed lemon juice
1 teaspoon freshly grated lemon rind
2 tablespoons chopped fresh mint, or 1 teaspoon dried mint

Heat the butter in a frying pan and add the pine nuts. Cook them over medium heat, stirring and turning them constantly, until lightly browned, about 2 or 3 minutes. Drain.

Put the lamb and olives into a large bowl.

Combine the dressing ingredients well in a small bowl.

Add the pine nuts to the lamb and olives and turn the dressing over the top. Combine well and season to taste with salt and pepper.

Arrange beds of spinach in equal portions on four dinner plates, spoon the salad equally on top, and sprinkle each salad with a little parsley. Serve immediately.

Serves 4

Greek Salad with Marinated Lamb Meatballs

A large, crisp, lusty Greek salad is one of my all-time favorites. Accented with lamb meatballs as a main course salad, it is even more inviting. Pita bread or crusty French or Italian bread and sweet butter should accompany the salad.

1 large head romaine lettuce, washed, dried, and torn into bite-sized pieces

1 medium-sized cucumber, cut into ¼-inch-thick slices
2 medium-large ripe tomatoes, cut into wedges
24 Greek olives
½ pound feta cheese, drained and cut into cubes
1 medium-sized red onion, thinly sliced and separated into rings

Lamb Meatballs:

¾ pound ground lamb
¼ cup plain bread crumbs
1 egg
½ teaspoon oregano
Salt and freshly ground pepper to taste
2 tablespoons olive oil
2 tablespoons vegetable oil

Dressing:

½ cup red wine vinegar
1 cup virgin olive oil
1 teaspoon minced garlic
½ teaspoon dried oregano
Salt and freshly ground pepper to taste

First, make the meatballs: Combine the lamb, bread crumbs, egg, and oregano and add salt and pepper to taste. Shape the mixture into little balls about 1 inch in diameter, cover, and chill for 30 minutes.

Heat the combined oils in a large frying

pan and cook the meatballs until done, shaking the pan often to brown them evenly, about 12 minutes. Drain and cool the meatballs.

Meanwhile, make the dressing: In a small bowl whisk the oil into the vinegar drop by drop, then add the garlic, oregano, and salt and pepper to taste and combine well.

Put the meatballs into a shallow dish and spoon half a cup of the dressing over them. Turn the meatballs to coat them evenly, and let rest at room temperature for 15 minutes.

To prepare the finished salad, arrange the ingredients on four individual dinner plates in the following order: First, make beds of romaine on each plate, then top with equal portions of cucumber slices, tomato wedges, olives, feta cheese, onion rings, and meatballs.

Whisk the dressing again and spoon it over the salads in equal amounts. Serve immediately.

Serves 4

Pork Tenderloin and Mushroom Salad

*T*his remarkably easy recipe brings out the pork's succulent flavor beautifully. Serve with baguette slices and sweet butter.

2 whole pork tenderloins
Salt and freshly ground pepper
⅓ cup peanut oil
7 tablespoons butter
1 bunch arugula, washed, dried, and stem ends trimmed (watercress can be substituted)
12 ounces thinly sliced mushrooms
1 medium-sized red onion, diced
8 sun-dried tomatoes, chopped
2 hard-boiled eggs, quartered

Dressing:

1 egg yolk, at room temperature
2 tablespoons red wine vinegar
1 tablespoon dry Marsala or Madeira
2 tablespoons freshly squeezed lemon juice
⅔ cup virgin olive oil
Salt and freshly ground pepper to taste

Season the pork tenderloins well with salt and pepper. Cut each tenderloin in half crosswise.

Heat the oil and 3 tablespoons of the

butter in a large frying pan and cook the pork over medium heat until browned on all sides. Reduce the heat to low and cook the pork, turning the pieces occasionally, until done, about 25 minutes. Drain and cool for 15 minutes.

Meanwhile, make the dressing. Whisk the egg yolk, vinegar, Marsala, and lemon juice together in a small bowl, drop by drop whisk in the olive oil, then season to taste with salt and pepper.

Heat the remaining 4 tablespoons of butter in a large frying pan and add the mushrooms. Cook over medium-high heat for 5 minutes, stirring often. Season lightly with salt and pepper and transfer to a colander. Let drain in the sink until ready to use.

Slice the pork crosswise into ⅛-inch medallions.

Cover the bottom of each of four dinner plates with the pork medallions and top the pork with equal amounts of the arugula, mushrooms, red onion, and sun-dried tomatoes.

Whisk the dressing again, spoon equal amounts of it over each salad, and garnish each salad with two hard-boiled egg quarters.

Serves 4

Curried Pork and Peach Salad with Sautéed Cashew Nuts

I first tasted warm sautéed cashew nuts in Kenya, which is famous for its plump, delectable cashews, arguably the world's most delicious and subtle-tasting nut. Since then I've been adding sautéed cashew nuts to various different salads (see recipe page 133, for example). They make a particularly wonderful addition to this interesting salad of combined pork, succulent juicy peaches, and creamy curried dressing.

2 tablespoons peanut oil
1 cup raw cashew nuts
3 cups cubed cooked pork tenderloin or boneless loin of pork
2 cups sliced ripe skinned peaches
½ cup diced cored and seeded red bell pepper
¼ cup thinly sliced scallion
4 cups shredded Chinese lettuce

Curried Mayonnaise III:

½ cup mayonnaise or Classic Mayonnaise (page 128)
½ cup sour cream
2 tablespoons honey

1 tablespoon apple cider vinegar or to taste
1 tablespoon curry powder
Salt and freshly ground pepper to taste

Heat the oil in a medium-sized frying pan and cook the cashew nuts for a few minutes over medium-high heat, stirring and turning often, until lightly toasted. Drain.

Combine the pork, peaches, pepper, and scallions in a large bowl.

Make the dressing: Whisk together the mayonnaise, sour cream, honey, vinegar, and curry powder and season it to taste with salt and pepper.

Turn the dressing over the salad and gently combine.

Arrange equal amounts of the lettuce on four dinner plates, spoon the salad on top of the lettuce in equal amounts, and sprinkle with the sautéed cashew nuts. Serve immediately.

Serves 4

Pork and Black Bean Chili Salad with Cheese and Green Chili Quesadillas

An uncommon and interesting chili salad, this dish is excellent in all seasons. Serve it with margaritas or limeade in summer, and Bloody Marys in the winter.

3 tablespoons olive oil
2 cups lean pork shoulder, cut into 1-inch cubes
½ cup chopped yellow onion
2½ cups cooked (1 cup dried beans) or canned black beans, drained
½ cup diced cored and seeded green bell pepper
1 cup diced seeded tomato
3 tablespoons diced red onion
1 cup sour cream

Dressing:

3 tablespoons freshly squeezed lime juice
2 tablespoons red wine vinegar
¾ cup virgin olive oil
1 tablespoon chili powder
1 teaspoon ground cumin
Salt and freshly ground pepper to taste

Heat the olive oil in a large frying pan and cook the pork over medium heat for about 10 minutes, turning often, until golden brown and tender. Remove from the pan and drain. Add the yellow onions to the pan and cook for 5 minutes, stirring often.

Put the pork and onions into a large bowl with the black beans, green pepper, tomato, and red onions and combine.

Make the dressing: Whisk together the lime juice and wine vinegar, drop by drop whisk in the olive oil, add the chili powder, cumin, and salt and pepper to taste, and combine well.

Pour the dressing over the salad, toss, and taste for seasoning. Cover and chill.

Thirty minutes before serving the salad, make the quesadillas and serve hot with the salad. Pass the sour cream.

Serves 4

Cheese and Green Chili Quesadillas

4 8-inch flour tortillas
1 cup shredded Monterey Jack cheese
¾ cup chopped green chilis

Preheat the oven to 350°.

Put two of the flour tortillas on a baking sheet and sprinkle the cheese evenly over the surface areas. Top with equal amounts of the green chilis. Top each with a flour tortilla and press them together slightly.

Bake for about 15 minutes, or until the cheese has melted. Cut into wedges and serve hot.

Makes 12 wedges

SEAFOOD SALADS

*I*n Taormina, Sicily, my husband and I had a glorious fresh mixed seafood salad, laced with virgin olive oil and lemon juice and served with plenty of dense Italian bread to soak up every drop of the delicious dressing. Mixed Seafood Salad in Roasted Red Peppers is my version of that memorably simple seaside lunch.

Seafood salads are among the world's most exquisite salads: rich in individual flavor, nutritious, low in calories, and uncomplicated. The freshness of the seafood is essential, of course. Today's quality fishmongers offer a multitude of daily selections, from overnight or early-morning catches from local waters to seafood that is flown in from all ports of the world. Frozen seafood should be avoided unless fresh is unavailable.

The fewer ingredients that are added to a seafood salad, the better. All that's really necessary is a well-constructed dressing to moisten and enliven the predominating flavor of the seafood.

An example of an incredibly good fresh fish salad is Fresh Poached Salmon and Green Pea Salad, which combines two foods that are classically served side by side. This dish is a lovely classic main course entrée for a July 4th celebration.

Chinese Shrimp Salad and Shrimp Salad with Honey-Mustard Dressing, two wonderful salads, are terrific any time of the year. They are both amazingly easy to prepare and can be made several hours in advance, which means that they are good choices for entertaining.

Of course, the ultimate main course salad ingredient is lobster, and I include a variation on the classic lobster salad with an unexpected twist—the addition of diced fresh fennel. Two other excellent salads using lobster can be found in the fruit chapter and the potato and rice chapter.

Most seafood is expensive, but there are first-rate exceptions. Mussels, for example, are inexpensive and make fine salads. The Mussel Salad with Basil Mayonnaise recipe included here was inspired by a wonderful creamy mussel salad once sampled in Puerto de Pollensa, Mallorca. Parsley was featured in that salad, but it is successfully replaced with fragrant fresh basil.

Much maligned canned white-meat tunafish is another great vehicle for seafood salad-making. Its texture and consistency hold up well and its flavor holds its own against that of any fish. Tuna, Feta, Black Olive, and Anchovy Salad is an excellent canned tunafish salad. In the pasta chapter, Curried Tuna and Radiatore Salad is another example of the transformation of this humble fish into a marvelous main course salad.

RECIPES

Mixed Seafood Salad in Roasted Red Peppers
Fresh Poached Salmon and Green Pea Salad
Tuna, Feta, Black Olive, and Anchovy Salad
Salade Niçoise with Grilled Tuna
Lobster and Fennel Salad on Spinach with Fried Onion Rings
Crab Meat and Tomato with Red Pepper Mayonnaise
Mussel Salad with Basil Mayonnaise
Chinese Shrimp Salad
Shrimp Salad with Honey-Mustard Dressing
Avocados Stuffed with Shrimp and Citrus Salad
Shrimp with Vegetables and Guacamole Salad
Sea Scallop and Grapefruit Salad
Tuna, Banana, and Walnut Salad

Mixed Seafood Salad in Roasted Red Peppers

A lemony mixture of marinated fresh squid, mussels, shrimp, and scallops stuffed in roasted red pepper shells makes a spectacular presentation. This goes well with Ratatouille Salad (page 156—omit the sausage) and Italian bread.

4 very large red bell peppers, with squared
bottoms (opposite the stem ends), enabling
them to stand up
3 tablespoons olive oil
1 pound small squid, cleaned, skinned, and
washed, the bodies cut into rings and the
tentacles chopped (a fishmonger can do this)
½ pound bay scallops, rinsed and dried, or
cubed sea scallops
1 quart shelled steamed mussels (page 182)
¾ pound boiled shelled deveined medium shrimp
(page 184), chopped
1 medium-sized red onion, chopped
3 tablespoons chopped fresh parsley

Dressing:
3 tablespoons freshly squeezed lemon juice or as
needed

1 garlic clove, minced
½ cup virgin olive oil
Salt and freshly ground pepper to taste

Cut the tops off the peppers and core and seed the insides, leaving the whole pepper intact. Lay the peppers on their sides on a baking rack over a pan, put the pan under the broiler so that the peppers are about 6 inches from the heat, and cook, turning often, until the sides blacken and begin to blister. Be careful not to burn the peppers. It takes about 5 minutes per side. When cool enough to handle, peel off and discard the skins and set the peppers aside.

Heat the olive oil in a large frying pan and cook the squid and scallops for about 2 minutes. Immediately remove from the heat and transfer to a large bowl.

Add the mussels, shrimp, onion, and parsley to the bowl and gently combine.

To make the dressing, combine the lemon juice, garlic, and olive oil in a jar, season to taste with salt and pepper, and shake well. Pour the mixture over the salad and toss.

Stuff the peppers with the salad and put into a dish just large enough to hold them, standing up. Cover and refrigerate for at least 3 hours. Serve cold.

Serves 4

Fresh Poached Salmon and Green Pea Salad

Nothing should interfere with the exquisite harmony of the flavors of the salmon and green peas. Only mayonnaise, a little lemon juice, and salt and pepper are added to enhance and bind the salad. Serve with toasted French bread slices and sweet butter, and chilled dry white wine.

2 stalks celery, sliced
1 carrot, sliced
1 bay leaf
6 sprigs parsley, tied in a bunch with kitchen string
½ cup dry white wine
2½ cups water
4 1-inch-thick salmon steaks
1¼ cups fresh green peas, cooked and drained

Dressing:

¾ cup mayonnaise or Classic Mayonnaise (page 128)
2 teaspoons freshly squeezed lemon juice
Salt and freshly ground pepper to taste

Put the celery, carrot, bay leaf, parsley, white wine, and water into a large frying pan and bring to a boil.

Add the salmon steaks, cover, and simmer for 10 minutes. Carefully turn each steak, recover, and simmer 10 minutes longer. Remove the salmon, drain, and cool.

Put the peas into a large bowl.

Remove the skin and bones from the salmon, flake the salmon, and put it into the bowl with the peas.

Combine the mayonnaise and lemon juice in a small bowl and season to taste with salt and pepper. Turn over the salad and combine gently. Serve immediately.

Serves 4

Tuna, Feta, Black Olive, and Anchovy Salad

*T*he combination of tuna, anchovies, and capers is responsible to a large extent for the exquisite marriage of flavors in the classic Italian sauce for *vitello tonnato*. Here, along with feta cheese, black olives, shallots, and cherry tomatoes, the three turn into a robust salad on their own. Serve with peeled cucumber slices and toasted pita bread with sweet butter.

8 ounces feta cheese, drained and cubed
20 giant pitted black olives, halved
20 cherry tomatoes, halved
1 2-ounce can anchovy fillets, drained and coarsely chopped
2 6½-ounce cans solid white-meat tuna packed in oil, well-drained and flaked

Shallot and Caper Dressing:

3 tablespoons red wine vinegar
3 shallots, minced
½ cup virgin olive oil
2 tablespoons capers
Salt and freshly ground pepper to taste

Put all the salad ingredients except for the tuna into a large bowl and toss.

To make the dressing, combine the vinegar and shallots in a small bowl, whisk in the oil drop by drop, stir in the capers, and season to taste with salt and pepper.

Pour the dressing over the salad and toss. Then add the tuna and gently combine. Serve immediately.

Serves 4

Salade Niçoise with Grilled Tuna

*T*he Salade Niçoise we serve most often for lunch or dinner, indoors or *al fresco*, is composed on a large platter with individual groupings of the ingredients so that each diner can select favored foods. My husband grills the thin tuna steaks on the outdoor grill or under the broiler just before we sit down to eat. The tuna is presented on its own platter and served with the main salad composition. Extra dressing and the peppermill are passed along with crusty bread and sweet butter.

1 medium-sized head romaine lettuce, washed,
    dried, and torn into bite-sized pieces
2 hard-boiled eggs, quartered
2 firm ripe tomatoes, cut into wedges
24 black Niçoise olives
12 rolled anchovy fillets with capers
1 yellow or red bell pepper, cored, seeded, and
    cut into ¼-inch-thick strips
1½ pounds cooked new potatoes, peeled and
    thinly sliced
1 10-ounce package frozen artichoke hearts,
    cooked and drained
1 pound green beans, cooked and cut into
    1-inch lengths
1½ pounds tuna, cut into ½-inch-thick steaks
Mayonnaise as needed

Dressing:

½ cup red wine vinegar
1 garlic clove, minced
1 egg yolk, at room temperature
1 tablespoon Dijon mustard
1 cup extra-virgin olive oil
Salt and freshly ground pepper to taste

Line a large ceramic serving platter with the lettuce.

Arrange the eggs, and all the ingredients through the green beans in individual rows across the lettuce. Cover and refrigerate.

To make the dressing, whisk the vinegar, garlic, egg yolk, and mustard together in a small bowl; drop by drop whisk in the olive oil; then season to taste with salt and pepper. Let rest at room temperature until ready to use.

Fifteen minutes before serving, heat the grill or broiler; lightly brush each side of the tuna steaks with mayonnaise. (This will keep them very moist and help prevent them from sticking to the grill.) Grill or broil them about 3 or 4 minutes on each side and transfer to a serving dish.

Spoon half of the dressing over the composed salad and serve the remaining half of the dressing in a bowl. Pass the tuna and peppermill.

Serves 4

Lobster and Fennel Salad on Spinach with Fried Onion Rings

*B*asic lobster salad made moist with good mayonnaise and lemon juice and seasoned only with salt and pepper is without question a wonderful salad. Served with fresh young greens, sliced ripe tomatoes, and freshly cooked potato chips it makes a fabulous meal. For a change, however, here's a lovely version of lobster salad with just a hint of Pernod and diced fennel, served on young spinach leaves, with tomato slices and a nest of crisp, freshly fried thin onion rings. Accompany with French bread and dry white wine or champagne.

6 quarts water
4 1½-pound live lobsters
¾ cup Classic Mayonnaise (page 128) or as needed
¼ cup diced fresh fennel
1 tablespoon freshly squeezed lemon juice
1 teaspoon Pernod
3 tablespoons heavy cream
Salt and freshly ground pepper to taste
½ pound young spinach leaves, washed, dried, and stemmed
4 medium-sized ripe tomatoes, sliced
1 recipe Fried Onion Rings

Bring the water to a boil in a lobster pot or other large pot. Immerse the lobsters in the boiling water, head first, one at a time. Cover, bring the water back to the boil, and cook the lobsters for 15 minutes. Drain the lobsters and cool.

Remove the lobster meat from the claws, tail, and shells. (Save the green tomalley, or liver, and orange roe, or lobster coral, of the female and serve in small bowls, if de-sired.) Cut the lobster meat into bite-sized pieces or medallions.

In a large bowl combine the mayonnaise, fennel, lemon juice, Pernod, and heavy cream. Add the lobster and combine. Season to taste with salt and pepper. Cover and chill for at least 1 hour before serving.

About 20 minutes before serving the salad, make the onion rings.

Arrange the spinach leaves in equal amounts on four dinner plates, top with the cold lobster salad, and garnish with the to-mato slices and onion rings.

Serves 4

Fried Onion Rings

8 cups thinly sliced small yellow onions (about 3½ pounds whole onions)
1 quart peanut or vegetable oil

Heat the oil in a French fryer or a 3½-quart heavy saucepan with at least 5-inch straight sides to 370°. Plunge half of the onions into the oil and cook until golden brown, about 4 minutes, stirring often. Re-move the onions, drain them, and season lightly with salt.

Cook the remaining half of the onions in the same manner. Serve warm.

Makes 2 cups

Crab Meat and Tomato with Red Pepper Mayonnaise

*T*oasted garlic bread (page 155) complements this salad nicely.

1 pound cooked lump crab meat, flaked
4 medium-sized tomatoes, peeled, seeds and pulp
*   removed, cut into ¼-inch-wide strips*
Salt and freshly ground pepper to taste
4 large Boston lettuce leaves, washed and dried
2 teaspoons freshly snipped chives

Red Pepper Mayonnaise:

2 tablespoons butter
1 tablespoon vegetable oil
1 large red bell pepper, cored, seeded, and
*   coarsely chopped*
1 cup mayonnaise or Classic Mayonnaise
*   (page 128)*
1 teaspoon Dijon mustard
1 teaspoon freshly squeezed lemon juice

Combine the crab meat and tomato in a large bowl and refrigerate.

To make the mayonnaise: Heat the butter and oil in a medium-sized frying pan and add the red pepper. Cook over medium heat for 10 minutes, stirring often. Puree the red pepper in a food processor and force it through a sieve or strainer. Combine the pureed red pepper, mayonnaise, mustard, and lemon juice.

Turn the mayonnaise over the crab meat and tomatoes, and combine thoroughly. Season to taste with salt and pepper.

Put a lettuce leaf on each of four dinner plates, spoon equal amounts of the salad on top, and sprinkle with the chives.
Serves 4

Mussel Salad with Basil Mayonnaise

*O*n a hot summer's day, this lovely aromatic salad served with tomato wedges, bell pepper strips, French bread slices spread with butter and toasted, and dry white wine makes a refreshingly light meal.

1 cup dry white wine
¼ cup chopped shallot
1 cup water
2 quarts mussels, scrubbed, debearded, and
*   rinsed just before cooking*

¼ cup minced pimiento
¼ cup diced celery hearts
¼ cup diced red onion
8 large Boston lettuce leaves, washed and dried

Basil Mayonnaise:

1 large egg yolk, at room temperature
2 teaspoons freshly squeezed lemon juice
½ cup olive oil
¼ cup finely chopped fresh basil
½ cup mayonnaise or Classic Mayonnaise (page 128)
Salt and freshly ground pepper to taste

Bring the wine to a boil in a large pot with the shallots and the water. Add the mussels, stir, cover, and cook exactly 5 minutes. Stir the mussels again, recover, and cook for 1 minute. Drain the mussels, discarding any that haven't opened.

Remove the mussels from their shells and put them into a large bowl.

To make the basil mayonnaise, whisk the egg yolk and lemon juice together, drop by drop whisk in the oil, add the basil and mayonnaise and whisk thoroughly, then season to taste with salt and pepper.

Add the pimiento, celery, and onion to the mussels, turn the mayonnaise over the salad, and combine well. Cover and refrigerate for 1 hour.

Arrange two lettuce leaves on each of four dinner plates and spoon the salad onto them in equal portions. Serve immediately.
Serves 4

Chinese Shrimp Salad

Serve this spectacular salad with cooked broccoli spears tossed in sesame oil.

2 pounds raw large shrimp, shelled and deveined
3 tablespoons peanut oil
⅓ cup tomato paste
3 tablespoons dry sherry
2 tablespoons soy sauce
1 tablespoon red wine vinegar
3 tablespoons honey
2 tablespoons chili paste
½ teaspoon crushed Szechuan pepper (available in Oriental and specialty food shops)
2 tablespoons freshly grated ginger
½ cup diced water chestnuts
¼ cup thinly sliced scallion
3 cups finely shredded iceberg lettuce
⅓ cup chopped roasted peanuts

Cut each shrimp in half lengthwise. (When shrimp are cut in this manner, they curl up when cooked, producing a very attractive corkscrew shape.)

Heat the oil in a wok or large frying pan with curved sides, and stir-fry the shrimp for 2 minutes. Remove pan from heat.

Combine the remaining ingredients except for the lettuce and peanuts, and add to the pan with the shrimp.

Toss the shrimp in the mixture and cook for 2 or 3 minutes over high heat until the sauce thickens slightly.

Cool, cover, and refrigerate the shrimp with the sauce for at least 1 hour before serving (the salad can be kept for several hours).

Just before serving, arrange a bed of the lettuce over the bottom of a serving platter. Retoss the shrimp, spoon over the lettuce, and sprinkle with the peanuts.
Serves 4

Shrimp Salad with Honey-Mustard Dressing

*P*repared in minutes, this remarkably good salad can easily be doubled. Because the dressing is so versatile, the shrimp can be replaced with 3½ cups of cooked cubed chicken or turkey. Serve with a green vegetable, such as asparagus, or a small mixed green salad, and French bread and sweet butter.

2 pounds raw medium shrimp, shelled and
    deveined
1 lemon, quartered

Honey-Mustard Dressing:
½ cup Dijon mustard
⅓ cup honey
¼ cup mayonnaise or Classic Mayonnaise
    (page 128)
2 tablespoons chopped fresh parsley

Put the shrimp with the lemon quarters into a saucepan. Cover them with water and slowly bring to a boil. Immediately reduce the heat and simmer for 3 minutes. Drain, run cold tap water over the shrimp for a minute, and drain well.

Combine the dressing ingredients in a large bowl with a wire whisk. Add the shrimp and toss. Cover and refrigerate for 1 hour. Toss again before serving.
Serves 4

Avocados Stuffed with Shrimp and Citrus Salad

This wonderful shrimp and citrus filling as well as many other stuffings like Tuna, Banana, and Walnut Salad (page 187), Green Goddess Chicken Salad (page 130), and Tabouli with Minced Lamb (page 23) complement avocado's velvety, subtle flavor. When avocados are in season, consider these and your own creative fillings. Serve with toasted French bread (pain grillé) if desired.

1 pound cooked medium-sized shelled and deveined shrimp (page 184)
1 pink grapefruit, peeled including white pith, cut into individual sections, and seeded
2 navel oranges, peeled including white pith, cut into individual sections, and seeded
2 large ripe avocados, halved and pitted

Citrus Dressing:

⅔ cup mayonnaise or Classic Mayonnaise (page 128)
2 tablespoons frozen grapefruit concentrate, thawed
⅛ teaspoon curry powder
2 teaspoons freshly squeezed lemon juice or to taste
2 tablespoons honey

Put the shrimp and grapefruit and orange sections into a large bowl and gently combine.

Combine the dressing ingredients with a wire whisk. Turn the dressing over the shrimp and fruit and toss.

Spoon equal amounts of the salad into the cavity of each avocado half in equal portions and serve immediately.

Serves 4

Shrimp with Vegetables and Guacamole Salad

Proponents of contemporary salad-making, salads minus the greens, will enjoy the combination here of cold poached shrimp on a palette of guacamole and marinated vegetables.

24 raw jumbo shrimp, shelled and deveined
1 lemon, halved and seeded
Dash of salt

¼ *cup thinly sliced scallion*
¾ *cup diced seeded tomato*
½ *cup cooked corn kernels*
½ *cup diced peeled and seeded cucumber*
1 *cup diced red cabbage*
⅓ *cup olive oil*
¼ *cup red wine vinegar*
Freshly ground pepper to taste
1 *recipe Guacamole*

Put the shrimp, juice from one lemon half, and the salt in a saucepan and cover with water. Slowly bring the water to a boil. Reduce the heat and simmer for 5 minutes.

Drain the shrimp and put them on a plate in a single layer. Squeeze the juice from the remaining lemon half over the shrimp, cover, and refrigerate.

Combine the scallions and vegetables in a bowl. In another bowl whisk the oil drop by drop into the vinegar and season to taste with salt and pepper. Pour over the vegetables and combine well. Cover and let marinate at room temperature for 1 hour, tossing after 30 minutes.

Just before serving the salad, make the guacamole and spread in equal amounts over each of four dinner plates. Pat the shrimp dry and arrange them on top of the guacamole in a circle around the edge, six per plate.

Drain the marinated vegetables well,

spoon equal amounts into a mound in the center of each plate, and serve immediately.
Serves 4

Guacamole

2 *ripe medium-sized avocados, peeled, pitted, and cubed*
2 *teaspoons chopped fresh cilantro (coriander)*
3 *tablespoons grated onion*
1 *garlic clove, chopped*
Dash or two of Tabasco or to taste
¼ *cup chopped peeled and seeded tomato*
1 *tablespoon freshly squeezed lemon juice*
Salt and freshly ground pepper to taste

Put all the ingredients in the blender and puree until smooth. Taste for seasoning and serve immediately.
Makes about 1¾ cups

Sea Scallop and Grapefruit Salad

*H*ere is my husband's favorite salad, which I serve with toasted bagel chips.

4 tablespoons sweet butter
⅓ cup chopped hazelnuts
1 pound sea scallops, rinsed, dried, and cut
    crosswise into ¼-inch-thick slices
2 large grapefruit, peeled including white pith,
    cut into sections, and seeded (do not
    substitute canned grapefruit)
1½ cups chicory (curly endive) pieces, washed
    and dried
1½ cups watercress leaves, washed, dried, and
    stems trimmed
1½ cups young arugula leaves, washed and
    dried

Hazelnut Oil Dressing II:

3 tablespoons red wine vinegar
1 teaspoon Dijon mustard
⅓ cup hazelnut oil
¼ cup olive oil
Salt and freshly ground pepper to taste

Heat the butter in a large frying pan and cook the hazelnuts over medium heat for 1 minute, stirring constantly. Remove the nuts with a slotted spoon and drain.

Immediately add the scallop medallions and cook for 1 minute. Turn the scallops, cook 1 more minute, and remove from the heat.

On each of four dinner plates, arrange the scallops and grapefruit sections in equal portions on opposite sides of each plate, leaving the center for the greens.

Combine the greens in a bowl.

To make the dressing, whisk together the vinegar and mustard, drop by drop whisk in the oils, and season to taste with salt and pepper.

Pour dressing over greens and toss.

Arrange the greens in the center of each plate in equal amounts and sprinkle the salads equally with the hazelnuts. Serve at room temperature.

Serves 4

Tuna, Banana, and Walnut Salad

*T*he unusual blend of flavors in this tuna salad is unexpectedly refreshing, particularly on a hot summer's day. Complete the meal with iced tea, buttered whole wheat bread sprinkled lightly with pepper, and ice-cold watermelon.

2 6½-ounce cans white-meat tuna packed in
    oil, well-drained and flaked
½ cup mayonnaise or Classic Mayonnaise
    (page 128), or as needed

1 teaspoon freshly squeezed lemon juice
½ cup coarsely chopped walnuts
½ cup thinly sliced celery
1 cup diced firm ripe banana
Salt and freshly ground pepper to taste
16 sprigs watercress, washed and dried
16 cherry tomatoes

Combine the tuna, mayonnaise, and lemon juice in a large bowl. Add the walnuts and celery and combine well. Fold in the bananas gently and season to taste with salt and pepper.

Spoon equal amounts of salad on each of four plates and garnish each salad with four sprigs of watercress and four cherry tomatoes. Serve immediately.

Serves 4

Seasonal Menus for Entertaining with Main Course Salads

Summer

I. A SUMMER PICNIC AT THE SHORE FOR SIX

MENU

Peking Chicken Salad in Lettuce Cups (page 139)

Rice and Vegetable Salad with Shrimp (page 93)

Sesame Breadsticks   Sweet Butter

Iced Tea with Fresh Mint Sprigs

Sugared Sliced Peaches

Chocolate Chip Cookies

Whether your outing's destination is a sandy beach at the ocean, a picnic table under trees by a lake, or a grassy bank by a stream, this enticing menu, with two main dish salads that can be prepared in advance, will satisfy all. (The shrimp in the Rice and Vegetable Salad with Shrimp can be eliminated, if desired.)

To prepare the peaches, slice 6 large fragrant, ripe, but firm, peaches into a bowl. Sprinkle them lightly with granulated sugar, drizzle 1 tablespoon of lemon juice over them, and toss them gently. Store the peaches in a tightly covered container, and keep chilled until served.

Since the chicken salad is eaten in hand, you might want to bring along little packets of moist towelettes, unless water's nearby for easy rinsing.

II. A FOURTH OF JULY PARTY FOR TWELVE

MENU

Crudités with Tuna-Tarragon Dip

Beef Vinaigrette Salad (page 117)

Ratatouille and Sausage Salad (page 156)

Corn on the Cob   Sweet Butter

Fresh Sliced Tomatoes Garnished with Basil and Virgin Olive Oil

Blueberries and Cherries with Nutmeg Ice Cream (page 40)

July 4th usually means a festive gathering of friends and family. The holiday menu presented here celebrates seasonal vegetables and fruits, and features a substantial main course salad, Beef Vinaigrette, as well as a summer favorite, Ratatouille, which has been enhanced with sausage. Triple both recipes.

The tuna-tarragon dip is one of those fabulous *easy* crowd-pleasers. It's made by combining two 6½-ounce cans of white-meat tuna (drained) with 8 ounces of softened cream cheese, 1 tablespoon of lemon juice, and 1 tablespoon of chopped fresh tarragon (or 1 teaspoon dried tarragon) in a food processor. (The dip can be made a day in advance and kept refrigerated.)

Select any fresh vegetables for the crudités that are seasonally fresh, but pick ones that aren't used in the ratatouille—cauliflower, carrots, radishes, fennel, or cucumbers, for example.

The dessert is red, white, and blue, honoring the holiday. (Strawberries can be substituted for the pitted cherries.)

III. A SUMMER SUNDAY BRUNCH FOR EIGHT

MENU

Grilled Lamb and Green Bean Salad (page 166)

New Potato Salad

Marinated Peppers

Toasted Garlic Bread (page 155)

Fresh Lemonade

Fresh Fruit Pie à la Mode

Summer's all-too-few Sundays are made especially enjoyable by entertaining with a brunch. Summer brunches are particularly sensible for people who weekend in the country, because guests and hosts alike begin to head back to the city in the early evening. But serving Sunday brunch at noon, no matter where you are, will allow everyone an afternoon of freedom to pursue their own pleasures, whether that be a game of tennis, a visit to a museum, or leisurely reading the Sunday papers.

This no-fuss menu's entrée—Grilled Lamb and Green Bean Salad—is grilled outdoors.

Make your favorite mayonnaise-based potato salad recipe using new potatoes. To prepare the marinated peppers, simply seed and core 2 large yellow, green, and red bell peppers each. Peel them with a vegetable peeler, thinly slice, and sprinkle with a combination of ⅓ cup of virgin olive oil, 2 tablespoons fresh lemon juice, 2 chopped anchovies, and freshly ground black pepper. Toss and chill until served. Double the Garlic Bread recipe.

Fall

I. AN ELEGANT CELEBRATION DINNER FOR SIX

MENU

Smoked Salmon with Capers

Lemon Wedges

Buttered Whole Wheat Bread Slices

Arugula Salad with Parmesan Cheese (page 63)

Pork Tenderloin and Mushroom Salad (page 169)

Hot-cooked Brussels Sprouts

California Chardonnay

Chocolate Mousse

It seems that there is always some event to celebrate when fall rolls around. The menu here features an example of an easily prepared new-style salad, Pork Tenderloin and Mushroom Salad (prepare the recipe with three pork tenderloins instead of two).

The recipe for the main course, Arugula Salad with Parmesan Cheese, contains salami and serves four, but since it's being used as a first course here, omit the salami; the other ingredients as given in the recipe will be sufficient in quantity.

II. A TV "TAILGATE" PARTY FOR SIX

MENU

Vegetable Salad Pizzas (page 103)

French Baguette Ham and Salami Heros

Iced Beer

Hot Fudge Sundaes

Surprise guests with the winning combination of individual piping hot Vegetable Salad Pizzas and French baguette heros. For the finale, serve the hot fudge sundaes at half time.

Make the heros out of 8-inch lengths of French baguettes spread lightly with softened sweet butter and filled with thinly sliced boiled ham, Genoa salami, and arugula or watercress leaves.

III. A PASTA SALAD TASTING PARTY FOR EIGHT

MENU

Bobbe Hart's Antipasto Pasta Salad (page 73)

Penne with Radicchio, Arugula, New Potatoes, and Fontina (page 70)

Fusilli and Shrimp with Lemon-Tarragon Dressing (page 81)

Crusty Italian Bread   Sweet Butter

Carafes of Dry White and Red Italian Wines

Italian Cheesecake

Everyone loves pasta. It's usually difficult to decide which pasta salad to serve at home or order in a restaurant because there are so many that seem tempting. Entertaining by having a pasta salad *tasting* will please everyone. Since each person will have a small serving of all three selections, the amounts of the recipes as given will be adequate for eight.

Winter

I. A DAY-AFTER-THANKSGIVING DINNER FOR FOUR

MENU

Curried Turkey and Wild Rice Salad (page 141)

Mango Chutney

French Bread   Sweet Butter

Chablis

Lemon Sorbet

Most of us are faced with leftover turkey on the Friday after Thanksgiving. This lovely curried turkey salad is quite simple to prepare. After a long day in the kitchen on Thanksgiving, an easy dinner is most welcome.

Lemon sorbet satisfies the sweet tooth, complements the meal, and is always refreshingly light, but if there is any pecan or pumpkin pie left over, by all means, serve that instead.

II. A NEW YEAR'S EVE SALAD BUFFET FOR TWELVE

MENU

Paella Salad (page 91)

Black Bean and Crunchy Vegetable Salad
(page 18)

Tossed Green Salad

Warm Whole Wheat Dinner Rolls   Sweet Butter

Dry White Spanish Wine

Coffee Ice Cream Balls Rolled in
Toasted Coconut

Chocolate Truffles

Champagne

Stilton Cheese   Crackers
Grapes   Walnut Halves
Port

New Year's Eve is one of the holidays when we find ourselves entertaining a crowd. A buffet of salads is a great menu problem solver. Because dinner in our household is served at 10:30 p.m., the menu is purposely on the light side, with no hors d'oeuvres required. Most guests will have snacked in the early evening, and you'll find they eat smaller amounts. For this reason

the Paella Salad and the Black Bean and Crunchy Vegetable Salad only need to be doubled, and they can be made in advance. Prepare a large mixed green salad with a tangy vinaigrette dressing, and toss the greens and dressing together just before serving dinner.

For the dessert, scoop 12 2½-inch balls out of 1 quart of coffee ice cream, quickly roll each in cooled toasted coconut, and immediately freeze the balls on a tray until served on dessert plates with truffles.

After dinner, serve champagne through midnight. Then, greet the new year with Stilton cheese, seedless grapes, and walnuts served with crackers, and pass the port.

III. VALENTINE'S DAY DINNER FOR TWO

MENU

Caviar   Toast Points

Champagne

Warm Duck and Sauerkraut Salad with
Raspberry Vinegar (page 147)

Buttered Green Peas

Ripe Brie

Fresh Pears

Several years ago I persuaded my husband to share a few ounces of caviar and a bottle of champagne with me on Valentine's Day instead of exchanging gifts. And since duck is a favorite food of ours, it's become a tradition on this special day, as well. Because I want to spend as little time in the kitchen as possible, I devised this marvelously quick Warm Duck and Sauerkraut Salad with a raspberry vinegar sauce and crisp duck cracklings.

Spring

I. A SPRING VEGETARIAN DINNER FOR EIGHT

MENU

Chinese Fried Walnuts (page 52)

Tomato Aspic Ring with Gazpacho Salad
(page 106)

Penne with Broccoli (page 76)

Crusty Italian Bread   Mozzarella

Muscadet

Sliced Navel Oranges with Strawberry Sauce

Sugar Cookies

A savory well-balanced menu need not contain meat or seafood at all, as illustrated by this delightful meal. Strict vegetarians can eliminate the mozzarella cheese and add 2 cups of cooked navy beans to the pasta salad for more protein. Other protein is supplied in the menu by the delicious, addictive Chinese Fried Walnuts. To serve the nuts to eight as an appetizer, cook 3½ cups of walnut halves as directed in the recipe on page 52; triple the other ingredients used in the recipe. The nuts can be prepared several days ahead and stored as directed.

II. A LIGHT SPRING DINNER FOR SIX

MENU

Melon, Berry, and Fig Salad in Prosciutto
(page 47)
Chinese Shrimp Salad (page 183)
Fresh-cooked Asparagus
Sparkling Mineral Water
Lemon Mousse with Gingersnaps

After winter's hearty warming fare, we begin to think of lighter foods in the spring for many reasons. Wonderful ingredients become available, like fresh berries and asparagus. We also suddenly become more weight-conscious as we begin shedding layers of clothing, and bathing suit weather approaches.

This menu includes many of my favorite foods, incredible rewards for cutting calories: berries, shrimp, asparagus, and lemons. Lemon mousse with gingersnaps, the dessert, is on the light side. All of these dishes offer a variety of flavors, colors, and textures.

Both the Melon, Berry, and Fig Salad in Prosciutto and the Chinese Shrimp Salad serve four, but they do not need to be increased to serve six because the former is used here as a first course and the latter is extended by the addition of asparagus.

III. BOX LUNCHES IN THE PARK FOR FOUR

MENU

Ziti and Green Vegetable Primavera Salad
(page 79)

Gorgonzola and Sliced Chicken Sandwiches
on Pumpernickel

Bloody Marys

Chocolate Brownies

The first few warm weekends of spring often send us happily off to our favorite park to bask in the sunshine and warm breezes. The occasion might be the season's first outdoor concert or an early softball game. Box lunches are fun to create, and conveniently transportable.

Pack everything in disposable containers, but provide pretty, oversized cloth napkins which can double as lap tablecloths.

Roquefort or blue cheese can be substituted for the Gorgonzola in the sandwiches.

INDEX